Alabama

ALABAMA BY ROAD

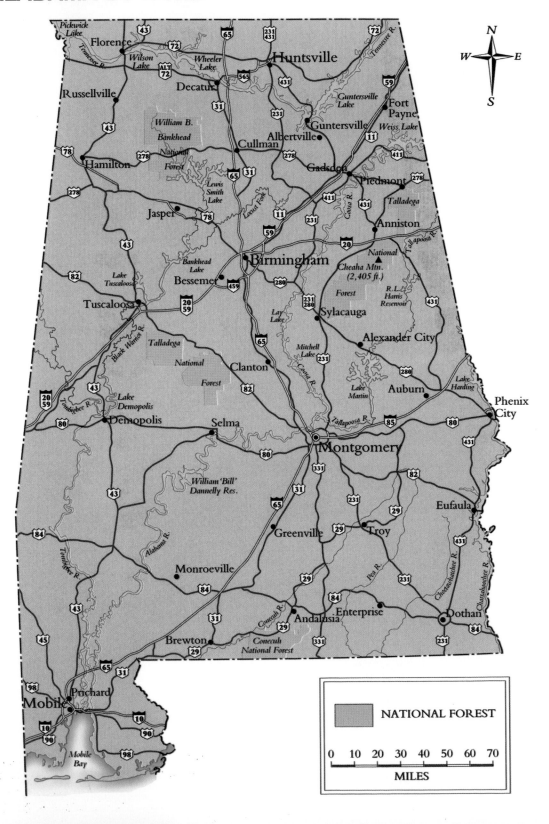

Celebrate the States

Alabama

David Shirley and Joyce Hart

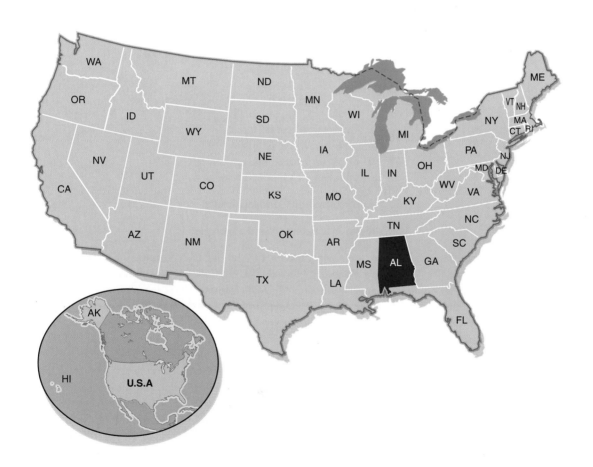

Marshall Cavendish
Benchmark
New York

Marshall Cavendish Benchmark
99 White Plains Road
Tarrytown, NY 10591-5502
www.marshallcavendish.us

Library of Congress Cataloging-in-Publication Data
Shirley, David, 1955–
Alabama / by David Shirely and Joyce Hart. — 2nd ed.
p. cm. — (Celebrate the states)
Summary: "Provides comprehensive information on the geography, history, wildlife, governmental
structure, economy, cultural diversity, peoples, religion, and landmarks of
Alabama"—Provided by publisher.
Includes bibliographical references and index.
ISBN 978-0-7614-3397-2
1. Alabama—Juvenile literature. I. Hart, Joyce, 1954– II. Title.
F326.3.S55 2009
976.1—dc22
2008004601

Editor: Christine Florie
Publisher: Michelle Bisson
Art Director: Anahid Hamparian
Series Designer: Adam Mietlowski

Photo research by Connie Gardner

Cover photo by Laurence Parent Photography

The photographs in this book are used by permission and through the courtesy of: *Corbis:* David
Muench, 11; Corbis, 16, 127; Robert Franz, 23; Flip Schulke, 60; Sam Sharpe, 64; Richard T. Nowitz,
71; Kevin Flemming, 80; John Springer Collection, 95; Mark Gibson, 104; David A. Northcott, 111;
Harris Barnes, 115; Bettmann, 120, 123, 129; Uriel Sinai/Pool, 131; *John Elk Photography,* 97;
Bridgeman Art Library: Inauguration of Jefferson Davis at Senate House, Montgomery, Alabama, 18th
February, 1861 (oil on canvas), Massolon, James (fl.1861)/Private Collection, Peter Newark Military
Pictures, 28; The Trail of Tears (oil on canvas), Lindneux, Robert Ottokar (1871-1970)/Woolaroc
Museum, Oklahoma, USA, Peter Newark Western Americana, 38; History class at the Negro Industrial
Institute at Tuskegee, Alabama, 1902 (b/w photo), American Photographer, (20th century)/Private
Collection, Peter Newark American Pictures, 48; *Digital Railroad.net:* 8, 25, 43; Murray Edwards, 21;
Jeff Haller, 103; *Art Life Images:* Jeff Greenberg, 54, 90; *AP Photo:* Dave Martin, 56, 79: Jay Reeves, 74;
John Godbey, 85; *The Image Works:* Jeff Greenberg, 12, 13, 18, 67, 94; Andre Jenny, 102; *Alamy:* Jeff
Greenberg, 19, 59, 70, 99, 117, 119, 134; David Sanger, 65; *Getty Images:* Altrendo Nature, 24; AFP, 88;
Michael Ochs Archive, 125; *Superstock:* age fotostock, back cover, 107 (T); Richard Cummins, 72; *Art
Archive:* Bibliotheque des Arts Decoratifs Paris/Gianni Dagli Orti, 31; *Age fotostock:* Jeff Greenberg,
82, 84, 92, 100; *Gibson Stock Photography:* 107 (B).

Printed in Malaysia
1 3 5 6 4 2

Contents

Alabama is a place of beautiful land and friendly people . . .

Alabama, your beautiful highways
Are carved through the mountains
Where loved ones do wait.
Alabama, your goldenrod flowers
And the welcome home sign
Hanging over the gate.
—from the song "Alabama," by Ira and Charlie Louvin

. . . who are willing to work hard, despite differences, to make Alabama a great state.

"There are more challenges to overcome. More problems to solve, and so much more we must do to make this state as strong as it can be. . . . Let us put Alabama and her people first."
—Bob Riley, governor of Alabama
State of the State Address, March 2007

Alabama is a place where tradition rules and time stands still . . .

"The present generation of people who had lived side by side for years and years, were utterly predictable to one another: they took for granted attitudes, character shadings, even gestures, as having been repeated in each generation and refined by time."
—from *To Kill a Mockingbird*, by Harper Lee

. . . but it is also a place that blends the past with the future.

"North Alabama offers so much to residents and visitors alike. . . . This area has the perfect combination of Old Southern charm and history blended with twenty-first-century, cutting-edge technology."
—Judy Ryals, President/CEO
Huntsville/Madison County Convention & Visitors Bureau

And Alabama is a place that if you leave, you long to return to.

"Sweet home, Alabama / Lord, I'm coming home to you."
—from the song "Sweet Home Alabama,"
by Edward King and Gary Rossington

"Alabama is my home, though I have spent much of my life outside her boundaries. But in the summer of 2007, while I was at a class reunion for Hicks Memorial High School in Autaugaville, I was reminded of the beauty of the people and the landscape of my home state. Now that I am getting ready to retire, Alabama's hills are calling me back home."
—Richard Ptomey, born in Autaugaville, Alabama

Alabama is one of those states whose landscape offers invigorating transformations, changing from mountain peaks in the north, to rolling pastureland in the center, to rich swamplands in the south that open up to salt breezes along the warm shores of the Gulf of Mexico. There is also the strong presence of history, which has brought waves of different cultures, from the American-Indian populations that were the first to see this land, to the French and Spanish who appeared at the birth of this state, to the African Americans who helped to build the new state, to the new surges of Hispanic and Asian residents who enhance the population today. From the cotton fields that have supported Alabama's economy in the past to the rocket development that brings promises of an exciting future, Alabama is a place where people know how to survive and prosper. It is no wonder that people who experience Alabama want to make it their home.

Chapter One

From Mountain to Shore

Alabama has one of the more varied landscapes of the southern states. At the northeastern corner is the heel of the Appalachian Mountains, marking the beginning of this great mountain chain that stretches the full length of the East Coast. Traveling south from this point, the Alabama landscape slowly levels out through a series of hills and valleys that eventually flatten and then dip into the warm waters of the Gulf of Mexico.

Depending on where people live or the areas people visit in this state, their impressions of what Alabama is can be wildly different. Some people think of the cool temperatures of the thick northern forests. Others have visions of swimming and fishing along the state's Gulf beaches. The majority of people know Alabama through its cities, while others think of Alabama as a thriving agricultural land. Alabama is all of this and more.

NORTH ALABAMA

North Alabama contains the southernmost part of the Appalachian Mountains, the great mountain range that stretches north to Maine. From this

The scenic Tennessee River Valley can be viewed from Gorham's Bluff at the top of Sand Mountain.

northeastern corner, flowing in a southerly direction, Alabama's landscape changes to a region of sandstone ridges, deep green valleys, and the high, winding hills of the Beaver Creek Mountains. Over the years mining companies searching for sandstone and limestone have blasted away some of the sides of ridges and hills in this area, leaving behind massive red-clay walls rising into the air where entire hills once stood. The towns of Gadsden, Scottsboro, Anniston, and Fort Payne are in this region.

Farther west is an area of flatlands and gentle, rolling hills. Sometimes these hills empty suddenly into deep ravines cut by the region's many rivers and streams. In Winston County in the northwest stands Natural Bridge, the longest natural rock archway east of the Rocky Mountains. This enormous sandstone and iron-ore bridge spans 148 feet. The walkway is 33 feet wide and 8 feet thick. Atop the bridge are the remains of a fossilized tree that is at least 4 million years old. The cities of Florence, Decatur, Madison, and Huntsville are located in this area.

Northern Alabama's most distinctive feature—maybe even more than the rolling hills and steep cliffs of the Appalachian Mountains—is the state's plentiful water. The entire northern portion of the state is dotted with rivers, streams, lakes, and waterfalls. At the center of it all is the majestic Tennessee River. The sprawling waters of the Tennessee wind their way westward across much of northern Alabama before twisting suddenly north to cut across the state of Tennessee. Alabama has no natural lakes, but engineers have dammed the Tennessee River at several of its bends to form large reservoirs and recreational lakes. These include Lake Guntersville and Wheeler and Wilson lakes, great locations to boat and fish.

The Tennessee River's countless tributaries have twisted and carved their way through the rock hills and limestone cliffs of northeastern Alabama to form an impressive network of caves, natural springs, and waterfalls.

Natural Bridge, a 148-foot natural walkway, is located in the Bankhead National Forest in Alabama.

These include DeSoto Falls, a spectacular 100-foot waterfall near Fort Payne. The elaborate system known as DeSoto Caverns is the site of a two-thousand-year-old American-Indian burial ground. The caves were discovered in 1540 by explorer Hernando de Soto and were mined during the Civil War for minerals needed to make gunpowder. During the Prohibition era, when federal laws prohibited the sale of liquor, bootleggers (people who made liquor illegally) stored their homemade concoctions, called moonshine, in the DeSoto Caverns.

The Tennessee River cascades down DeSoto Falls in a 100-foot drop.

Many of Alabama's caves have become popular with spelunkers (people who like to explore caves). Some of the more famous caves include Cathedral Caverns, outside of Woodville; Rickwood Caverns, north of Warrior; and Russell Cave, outside of Bridgeport. Russell Cave has become famous for the extensive artifacts found there, some possibly dating back ten thousand years.

Northern Alabama is made up of four distinct areas. Going from north to south, they are referred to as the Highland Rim, the Cumberland Plateau,

The Cathedral Caverns are a good place to explore Alabama's cave system.

LAND AND WATER

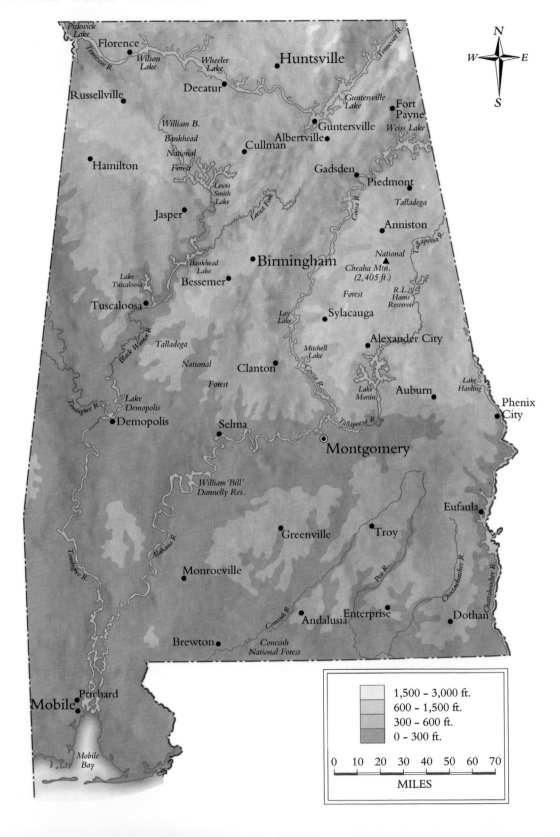

Pickwick Lake
Florence
Wilson Lake
Russellville
Wheeler Lake
Decatur
Huntsville
Tennessee R.
Tennessee R.
Guntersville Lake
Fort Payne
Weiss Lake
William B. Bankhead National Forest
Cullman
Guntersville
Albertville
Hamilton
Gadsden
Piedmont
Lewis Smith Lake
Talladega
Jasper
Locust Fork
Anniston
Tallapoosa R.
Bankhead Lake
Birmingham
National
Cheaha Mtn. (2,405 ft.)
Lake Tuscaloosa
Bessemer
Coosa R.
Forest
R.L. Harris Reservoir
Tuscaloosa
Lay Lake
Sylacauga
Black Warrior R.
Talladega
Mitchell Lake
Alexander City
National
Clanton
Coosa R.
Lake Harding
Tombigbee R.
Forest
Lake Martin
Auburn
Phenix City
Lake Demopolis
Demopolis
Selma
Tallapoosa R.
Montgomery
William 'Bill' Dannelly Res.
Eufaula
Greenville
Troy
Tombigbee R.
Alabama R.
Monroeville
Pea R.
Chattahoochee R.
Choctawhatchee R.
Conecuh R.
Enterprise
Dothan
Andalusia
Brewton
Conecuh National Forest
Prichard
Mobile
Mobile Bay

	1,500 – 3,000 ft.
	600 – 1,500 ft.
	300 – 600 ft.
	0 – 300 ft.

0 10 20 30 40 50 60 70

MILES

the Appalachian (or Alabama) Ridge and Valley, and the Piedmont Upland. The Highland Rim is located in the northwestern corner of the state. The majority of the Highland Rim area also encompasses the Tennessee River Valley. Farming is prevalent there, taking advantage of the fertile valley soil.

The Cumberland Plateau is an almost level sandstone upland that runs along the western side of the Appalachian Mountains, from Kentucky down to Alabama. It averages about 1,300 feet in elevation.

South of the plateau is the Appalachian Ridge and valley region, which contains large deposits of coal, iron, and limestone, ingredients that have made this region a center for the manufacture of steel. The Coosa River drains this section of the state.

The southernmost of the regions of northern Alabama is the Piedmont Upland, an area of hills and fertile valleys. The Piedmont is another landform that spreads north over much of the East Coast, from Alabama to New Jersey. In Alabama the Piedmont is home to much of the state's agricultural activity. Cheaha Mountain, Alabama's highest point, standing at 2,407 feet above sea level, is also located there.

According to the Alabama Forestry Commission, 71 percent of Alabama's landscape is covered in forests. Although most of the forest is privately owned, there are several national forests. Two of them are located in the north: Bankhead National Forest in the northwest corner of the state and the Talladega National Forest in the Piedmont Upland region.

SOUTH ALABAMA

In contrast to the rolling hills and hardwood forests of northern Alabama, southern Alabama is covered primarily by flat, expansive meadows and farmlands, and dense pine forests. Much of the area sits on what is called the East Gulf Coastal Plain. This region of beaches, marshland, and sandy clay soil spreads north from the Gulf of Mexico toward the center of the state. A wide band of dark, sticky clay known as the Black Belt stretches east and west across the coastal plain. The Black Belt is home to the state's most productive farmland. Large cotton plantations once dominated this region.

Just south of the Black Belt, in the state's southwestern corner, dark soil has formed between the banks of the Mobile and Tensaw rivers. Known as the Mobile-Tensaw Delta, this long, fertile stretch of land was formed over thousands of years, as regular flooding deposited rich mud from the bottom of the rivers in thick layers along the shore.

A field of young cotton plants sprouts under the southern Alabama sun.

MOBILE BAY, AN ESTUARY

Mobile Bay, which opens at the southwestern part of the state into the Gulf of Mexico, is approximately 32 miles long and 23 miles wide at its widest point. It is through Mobile Bay that barges enter and continue north onto Alabama's vast river system to deliver goods. The bay basin is characterized by barrier islands, tidal marshes, cypress swamps, and oyster reefs. When freshwater from rivers mixes with saltwater from the sea, an estuary is formed. Alabama's Mobile Bay is an estuary that is the receiving basin for the sixth-largest river system in the United States. Estuaries and the marshy areas around them are home to abundant and divergent plant and animal life, including many species that can survive only in such mixed-water environments. Like other estuaries, Mobile Bay is an important home for some of Alabama's most interesting—and most endangered—species.

At home in Mobile Bay is a wide variety of wildlife that includes 49 species of mammals, 126 species of reptiles and amphibians, 337 species of freshwater and saltwater fish, 355 species of birds, as well as many different types of aquatic insects. For many species, such as shrimp, oysters, crabs, and mullet, Mobile Bay is a major nursery area of the northern Gulf of Mexico. During some part of their life cycle these sea creatures depend on the estuaries for food and protection.

In recent years chemicals from factories and farms (in the form of fertilizers) have polluted Alabama's estuaries, while lumber and land development have destroyed many inland swamps and forests. This and other practices have threatened the very survival of many plants and animals that need the mixed-water environment.

Alabama joined the Association of National Estuary Programs more than a decade ago to help improve Mobile Bay. Although this has made the state government as well as the general population more aware of pollution and its damaging effects on the bay, Mobile Bay continues to experience one of the highest rates of plant and animal extinctions in estuaries in the United States. Some progress has been made, but much more is needed.

Moving through the delta toward the city of Mobile and the Gulf Coast, the land becomes spotted with marshes, bayous, and swamps. These shallow, tree-filled waterways are formed when rivers overflow and flood low inland fields. Many of these fields remain submerged in water year-round. "Kids growing up down here love to pretend they're living in the jungle," explains a store owner in Mobile. "The tangle of tall reeds, ferns, and vines along the swamps are sometimes so thick you really do need a machete to cut your way through, and even the shallowest waters are home to water moccasins [snakes] and snapping turtles and alligators. It really can be an adventure just making your way along."

Swamp lakes containing hardwoods dripping with Spanish moss are found at Perry Lakes Park.

Farther south, the deep green swamplands recede into the sandy beaches that line Mobile Bay and the Gulf Shore. In the pale blue waters of the Gulf of Mexico, just south of the Alabama coast, two long, narrow islands— Pleasure Island and Dauphin Island—are the only remnants of a peninsula that once extended from the mainland's sandy beaches into the Gulf.

Southern Alabama has a rich supply of rivers. The largest are the Tombigbee, Alabama, Mobile, Tensaw, and Chattahoochee. As with the Tennessee River in the north, rivers in southern Alabama have been dammed to form lakes. These include Lake Eufaula and the Walter F. George Reservoir on the Chattahoochee River and the William "Bill" Dannelly Reservoir on the Alabama River.

Alabama's Gulf Coast has miles of sandy beaches.

Alabama has a subtropical climate, which means it has short, mild winters and long, hot, humid summers. There is little if any snowfall during the winter, except in the northern mountains. Low temperatures in the winter are frequently well above freezing. And in the summer the thermometer often reaches 100 degrees Fahrenheit. When Alabama's typically high humidity is factored in, summer days can feel even hotter.

On February 5, 2008, unusually warm winter temperatures spread across the southern states and as far north as Ohio. Temperatures broke records in such places in Alabama as Tuscaloosa, reaching into the 80s. As the warm air clashed with the more typical winter cold air across the rest of the country, a very strong system of storms developed, and the National Weather Service issued several tornado warnings. By the end of the day eighty-two tornadoes had been sited and confirmed.

RECORD TEMPERATURES

The highest temperature recorded in Alabama was 112 degrees Fahrenheit, recorded on September 5, 1925, at Centerville. The lowest temperature recorded in Alabama was –27 degrees Fahrenheit, recorded on January 30, 1966, at New Market.

Fierce thunderstorms and long, steady rains are common in the summer. The Gulf region is also a frequent target of hurricanes. Tornadoes are also known to whirl in during summer storms. The average annual rainfall in Alabama's coastal regions is 65 inches, with an average of 53 inches falling each year in the rest of the state.

The first tornado hit Arkansas. Another series of tornadoes devastated parts of Tennessee. Then around 1:00 AM (on February 6), tornadoes struck Lawrence County, Alabama, and moved across the state to Jackson County. A tornado that touched down in Huntsville had estimated wind speeds of 180 miles per hour.

In Prattville an estimated fifty people were injured, and at least two hundred homes were destroyed. In a story posted on MSNBC's Web site, Prattville resident Shannon Edwards is quoted as saying, "It sounded like a train came through my window." Edwards, who was nineteen years old, was rescued after being trapped under the debris of what remained of her house. "My whole bed just flipped up. I didn't know where I was going to end up. I didn't know what was going on."

Neighbors gather after the February 2008 tornadoes wreaked havoc in an Alabama neighborhood.

HURRICANES IN ALABAMA

Hurricane season in the United States begins on the first day of June and extends through the end of November. During this time, hurricanes are likely to form in the warm waters of the Caribbean and have the potential to make landfall in the states around the Gulf of Mexico and along the East Coast. Alabama usually gets its share.

Hurricane Camille, one of the strongest hurricanes to make landfall in the United States, struck in 1969 with wind speeds measuring an estimated 190 miles per hour. (This hurricane knocked out most wind-measuring devices, so exact measurements are not known.) Although Camille did not make a direct hit on Alabama, it caused extensive damage with both its strong winds and high storm surge (height of the water above normal high-tide levels), which averaged about 25 feet.

Developing in 1979, Hurricane Frederic had sustained winds of around 120 miles per hour and made a direct hit on Mobile Bay. Before smashing into Mobile, Frederic completely wiped out most structures in Gulf Shores. At the time, Frederic was declared one of the most damaging of all U.S. storms.

Developing in 2004, Hurricane Ivan had sustained winds of 120 miles per hour when it hit the shores of Alabama and brought with it a storm surge of 10 to 15 feet. Ivan ranks as the tenth most intense hurricane to make landfall in the United States.

In 2005, Hurricane Katrina, one of the most devastating U.S. storms ever, developed. It did not hit Alabama directly, but its winds spread wide across the southwestern part of the state, causing at least 120-miles-per-hour winds and storm surges of between 15 and 20 feet. Mobile was flooded with water that ran 5 feet high in the streets. Inland towns such as Atmore were severely damaged, and flooding was widespread across the state.

Trees cover more than two-thirds of Alabama. In the northern part of the state the hills and valleys are colored by both the deep green leaves of hardwood trees, such as hickory and oak, and the lighter green needles of softwood pine. The meadows and ridges of the coastal plain to the south are dominated by the loblolly, shortleaf, and longleaf southern pine.

The swamps and marshlands of the Mobile-Tensaw Delta and the Gulf Coast are filled with cypress, cedar, magnolia, live oak, and water oak. Thick drapes of Spanish moss (not really a moss but rather a bromeliad that lives on trees and gains its nutrients and water from the air) often hangs from the massive limbs of the thick, squatty oak trees.

Spanish moss thrives in the warm, moist Alabama air.

In the spring wild as well as cultivated azalea—with blossoms ranging from fragrant white to pink and orange—brighten the state. Along with the state flower, the camellia, Alabama's highways and back roads are dotted with the dazzling colors of goldenrod, aster, pink, Dutchman's-breeches, orchids, and southern camas.

The state's broad meadows, dense forests, and calm shores are filled with a rich variety of animals, including fox, white-tailed deer, mink, skunk, bobcat, squirrel, rabbit, and raccoon. Beaver can frequently be seen building enormous wooden dams at the edges of riverbanks and lakes and throughout the thick marshland of the Mobile-Tensaw Delta. Alligator are common in the swamps and bayous of southwestern Alabama.

Carnivorous pitcher plants bloom in an Alabama field during springtime.

The state's many birds include the bluebird, cardinal, blue jay, and mockingbird. The state bird, the yellowhammer, is a colorful member of the woodpecker family. The bird was named for the way it flashes the yellow underside of its wings as it hammers furiously against tree bark with its beak. During the Civil War, Confederate soldiers adopted the bird as a mascot because its yellow and gray feathers matched the colors of their uniforms. Hoping it would bring them good luck, soldiers from Alabama wore the bird's feathers in their hats as they marched into battle.

Bluebirds are a common sight in Alabama.

With its extensive waterways, Alabama also abounds in fish. Catfish, crappie, bream, drum fish, bull fish, and largemouth bass are common. The calm waters of Mobile Bay and the Gulf of Mexico are filled with a rich supply of fish and other forms of sea life, including flounder, mullet, red snapper, oyster, crab, and shrimp.

With Alabama's vast supply of wildlife, hunting and fishing are popular. Across the state hunters leave their homes before sunrise on weekend mornings to track duck, rabbit, white-tailed deer, quail, and the state's most popular game bird, wild turkey. Wild turkeys are among the most difficult animals to track and hunt. For one thing, the fleet-footed birds are shy and reclusive. Hunters are forced to wander into remote areas of the forest to find the birds' roosting places. Wild turkeys also blend in well with the natural colors in the woods and can easily scamper to safety beneath thickets and brush.

JUBILEE

Each year between June and September folks living south of Mobile take part in the state's strangest traditional fishing activity. For generations people from Spanish Fort, Daphne, and Fairhope have gathered during this event on the eastern shore of Mobile Bay, wading barefoot in the shallow waters for Jubilee. They come to the beach to await the arrival of great teams of fish, crab, and shrimp that are drawn to the site during the summer.

According to legend, many fish and crustaceans arrive each year, quickly becoming disoriented in the shallow waters and breaking waves on the shore. For a brief period the animals float helplessly in the backwash from the waves, and many of them wash up on shore. No one knows for sure which day the swarms of sea creatures will arrive. But local residents who are lucky enough to pick the right day to patrol the shore simply help themselves to all the fish, crabs, and shrimp they can carry away with them in the buckets and ice chests they brought from home.

Although the legend of Jubilee leaves a lot of questions unanswered, there is a scientific explanation for this phenomenon. According to the National Oceanic and Atmospheric Administration, oxygen depletion is the force that drives many aquatic animals into the shallow waters of Mobile Bay. This depletion of oxygen (or hypoxia) is caused by different factors, including the high temperatures of Alabama's late summer. Another major factor is the number of decomposing organisms in the water. Bacteria, fungi, and other decomposer organisms consume oxygen while they break down organic matter. Wastewater with great amounts of organic matter, such as that contained in sewage, also contribute to a lack of oxygen. Another factor is the amount of salt in the water. During calm weather very salty water accumulates and stagnates in the bay.

When there are low levels of dissolved oxygen in the water, aquatic animals become lethargic and move toward the estuary, where wave action supplies shallow water with more oxygen. Jubilees are thus caused by a movement of fish and crustaceans, which normally live along the bottom of the bay, to the top of the water, where they are then washed along the shore.

In the 1940s wild turkeys were hunted with such frequency that they almost disappeared from Alabama. Since that time the state has created special wildlife sanctuaries to protect the birds. Today, Alabama once again boasts one of the largest populations of wild turkeys in the nation. In certain areas the birds can often be seen congregating in small groups, wobbling nonchalantly along the roadside.

"The wild turkey is a lot like Alabama," explains a man living near Muscle Shoals. "It's not the fastest or the strongest bird in the woods, and it's certainly not the flashiest. But it's a proud bird and determined to survive. Try sneaking up on one. You think you're about to take it by surprise, and all of a sudden, it's ducked into a hollow or scampered through the brush. It's gone, just like that."

ALABAMA'S THREATENED AND ENDANGERED SPECIES

According to the U.S. Fish and Wildlife Service, Alabama has seventy-eight endangered or threatened animals. Most of these animals are endangered by pollution or the development of wild areas into suburbs and by overfishing. The threatened animals include the painted rocksnail, Red Hills salamander, loggerhead sea turtle, eastern indigo snake, Gulf sturgeon, gopher tortoise, and flattened musk turtle. The endangered animals include the gray bat, Alabama cavefish, Alabama beach mouse, hawksbill sea turtle, leatherback sea turtle, Alabama cave shrimp, armored snail, wood stork, red-cockaded woodpecker, and the humpback whale.

Chapter Two

Struggle and Change

Alabama has experienced many changes since achieving statehood in 1819. However, its history stretches thousands of years into the past.

FIRST INHABITANTS

People began living in what is now Alabama more than 12,000 years ago. At first these seminomadic Paleo-Indians (who entered what is today the United States sometime between 13,000 BCE and 7,900 BCE) lived along the Tennessee River in small groups that traveled according to seasons, supporting themselves by hunting, fishing, and gathering fruits and vegetables that grew in the wild. The Archaic Indians followed, living in Alabama between 2000 BCE and 500 BCE. In winter some of these early people found shelter in such places as Russell Cave. The Archaic Indians left mounds of shells in the Tennessee and Tombigbee river valleys and on Dauphin Island.

Eventually, some of these early peoples began to settle in larger, more permanent communities. These people began to clear some of the land in order to create fields in which to grow vegetables and fruits.

In early 1861 Jefferson Davis was inaugurated president of the Confederate States at the Senate House in Alabama.

This group flourished around 1300 CE, two hundred years before European explorers visited the area, and is referred to as the Mississippian culture. These people are remembered for creating a settlement that contained as many as three thousand people, a huge community for the times in North America. The people of this settlement lugged heavy bags of dirt on their backs from long distances away to build towering mounds on which they built homes for their leaders; they also used the mounds for burial grounds. Having homes on top of the mounds provided a clear view of the nearby Black Warrior River and other more distant areas from which enemies might arrive. The Mississippians also built a huge protective wall, 1 mile long and 12 feet high, around their settlement. Today, at Moundville Archaeological Park in central Alabama, visitors can walk through the South's largest example of a permanent American-Indian settlement. The park contains twenty-six preserved mounds.

Later settlements emerged as various other American-Indian groups set their roots in this area, including the Creek, Cherokee, Choctaw, Chickasaw, Apalachicola, Koasati, Mobilian, Osochi, Sawokli, Tohome, Tuskegee, Muskogee, and the group whose name would one day be adopted for the state, the Alibamu. The leaders of these groups would later greet—and often struggle against—the region's earliest European settlers.

EUROPEANS ARRIVE

The first Europeans to reach present-day Alabama were led by the Spanish explorer Alonso Álvarez de Piñeda, who sailed into Mobile Bay in 1519. He was searching the Gulf of Mexico for a sea route that would allow him to sail to Asia. He was also mapping the Gulf shoreline. There is no record of his

Many American-Indian groups, such as the Creek, settled in what is now Alabama.

landing in what would become Alabama, but he is credited with being the first European to at least see the shoreline.

In 1540 the Spaniard Hernando de Soto became the first European to explore the state's interior. De Soto and several hundred soldiers entered through the northeastern part of what would become Alabama and then marched and rafted southward down its entire length. De Soto was looking for gold. He and his men often used force or even enslaved members of the American-Indian population to pressure them into giving

up food and any information on where to find the gold that de Soto insisted was nearby. Needless to say, this enraged the American Indians, and de Soto's ruthless reputation began to precede him. De Soto was then met with more hostile behavior as he and his troops traveled on.

In October 1540 de Soto traveled farther south, where he met Tuscaloosa, the chief of the Mobilian Indians. Tuscaloosa was called the Black Warrior and stood at least a head taller than the rest of his people. He was about forty years old and was known for his bravery in battles. De Soto asked Tuscaloosa to join his soldiers in their march south to ensure

In 1540 Hernando de Soto explored the region that is now Alabama in search of gold.

protection for his soldiers. Although Tuscaloosa went along with de Soto's plan, the chief sent some of his men ahead of the de Soto party to inform his people in Mauvila (a Mobilian settlement somewhere north of present-day Mobile) that they were coming.

Upon their arrival in Mauvila, Tuscaloosa, sensing that he was considered de Soto's hostage, broke away from de Soto's men. Shortly after this one of de Soto's spies confirmed that thousands of Tuscaloosa's warriors, as well as numerous warriors from other tribes, were hiding in the village. Tuscaloosa warned de Soto that he had better leave. One of de Soto's men attacked a high-ranking chief, thus setting off one of the biggest battles of de Soto's journey. He was wounded during this battle.

Much of de Soto's army had not entered Mauvila with him but, hearing the sounds of battle, quickly came forward and knocked down the settlement's gates. The battle lasted nine hours, during which 82 Spaniards and an estimated 11,000 of Tuscaloosa's people were killed. The entire settlement was burned to the ground. Tuscaloosa is thought to have died in the fires.

Much of de Soto's supplies were lost in the fires, leaving his troops without medicine and food. De Soto's men set out to steal provisions from surrounding Indian settlements. Although de Soto learned that his ships were near and laden with food, he also heard rumors that his men wanted to abandon him and sail back to Spain. De Soto decided not to seek out the ships and instead instructed his troops to march northward.

However, word about the destruction of Mauvila had spread throughout the other American-Indian groups in the region. Everywhere de Soto and his men went, they were forced to fight for their passage.

At the Battle of Mauvila de Soto and his soldiers battled Chief Tuscaloosa and his warriors.

De Soto would eventually reach the Mississippi River and cross it, continuing his search for gold, although he would never find any. Later, in 1542, de Soto returned to the Mississippi, where he died at the age of forty-two.

More than 150 years after de Soto's journey, the first permanent European settlement was established in what is now Alabama. In 1702 two French-Canadian brothers, Pierre Le Moyne d'Iberville and Jean-Baptiste Le Moyne de Bienville, founded a settlement they called Fort Louis, located on the banks of the Mobile River. Unfortunately, in 1711 the river flooded, isolating the town that had grown up there. The French moved their settlement 27 miles downriver to the site of what is today Mobile. The brothers called this city La Mobile, and it served as the capital of French Louisiana until 1722, when New Orleans was chosen for that honor.

Beginning with de Soto's entrance, diseases brought by the Europeans decimated American-Indian communities. Thousands died, for the American Indians had no natural immunities against the diseases that Europeans had battled for ages. By the eighteenth century the American-Indian population regrouped into new and larger communities for a better chance of survival. The four major groups were the Cherokee (in the north), Creek (in the mid-Atlantic and southeast), Chickasaw (in the northwest), and Choctaw (in the southwest).

In the following years European powers fought in the French and Indian War (1756–1763) over a land area that included Alabama. Britain controlled the area that would become Alabama from 1765 to 1780. When the American colonies gained their independence from England in 1783, what would later become northern Alabama became part of the United States, while southern Alabama remained in the hands of the Spanish. In 1795 the United States acquired most of present-day Alabama from Spain. Only the Gulf Coast and the area around Mobile remained under Spanish rule.

During the War of 1812, in which U.S. forces fought against the British at several points on the continent, Alabama saw its own share of conflict. First, the United States put pressure on the Spanish living along Alabama's southern coastline and in April 1813 was able to annex the land in western Florida from the Pearl to the Perdido rivers. In the same month the Spanish were forced to surrender their command of Mobile. One year later, though, coveting the great southern port of Mobile, British forces attempted to capture the area by attacking Fort Bowyer on Mobile Point. But the British forces failed. Discouraged but not ready to give up, the British troops moved toward New Orleans, hoping for victory. However, they failed again. Still undaunted as they turned around and headed east, the British launched a second attack on Fort Bowyer in September 1815, and this time they succeeded. Unfortunately for the British, after earning this victory, they learned that the war was over and abandoned the captured fort.

During this period the Creek Indians joined with the British in an attempt to stop the alarmingly fast takeover of their lands by white settlers. Widespread attacks in present-day Alabama took place, because the Creek warriors hoped that in supporting the British, they might win back their homeland. This part of the War of 1812 came to be known as the Creek Indian War, which started with an uprising at Fort Mims, in Baldwin County. Almost all of the settlers within Fort Mims were killed.

In an effort to win their land back, the Creek joined with the British and held an uprising at Fort Mims, marking the beginning of the Creek Indian War.

Several battles were fought throughout what would become the state of Alabama between 1813 and 1814. There was great loss of life on both sides. General Andrew Jackson, knowing that the Creek were poorly organized due to conflicts among them, some wanting land and others peace, marched into Creek territory. In 1814 Jackson won a decisive battle at Horseshoe Bend in present-day Daviston. Then on August 9, 1814, the Creek were forced to cede 20 million acres of land to the U.S. government. This opened up almost half of present-day Alabama to more white settlers as the Creek and other American-Indian people were forced off their land.

EARLY STATEHOOD

In 1819 Alabama became the twenty-second state admitted to the Union. During its early years of statehood wealthy cotton planters from the Carolinas and Georgia began settling in Alabama. With the forced labor of thousands of African slaves, the white farmers cleared the land and built large plantations in the fertile Black Belt and Tennessee Valley.

Although not forced into slavery, Alabama's American Indians did not fare well in the early years of statehood. In 1838 the U.S. government,

Large cotton plantations developed during Alabama's early years as a state.

because of demands from settlers for more land, forced more than 16,000 Cherokee and members of other groups to leave their homes in Alabama, Tennessee, Georgia, and North Carolina. The government had set May 23, 1838, as the deadline for voluntary removal. Authorities hoped that the American-Indian people would leave their homelands on their own. However, as the deadline approached, officials saw that this would not be the case for everyone. President Martin Van Buren created a special military unit led by General Winfield Scott to command the forced removal of all American Indians still claiming their land in the designated states. Behind General Scott were seven thousand U.S. soldiers. The American Indians were forcibly removed at gunpoint and gathered into camps. One camp was located at Gunter's Landing in Guntersville, Alabama, located on the Tennessee River. The displaced people traveled approximately 1,200 miles mostly on foot, before ending up in what was called Indian Territory,

Robert Ottokar Lindneux depicts the 1838 removal of American Indians from their homeland in The Trail of Tears.

located in present-day Oklahoma. It is estimated that between two and six thousand people died on what is now known as the Trail of Tears.

Meanwhile, the dream of establishing a new cotton empire in Alabama was shattered when a series of droughts devastated many of the state's cotton farms. The young state faced one crisis after another. A nationwide depression, which began in 1837, led Governor Benjamin Fitzpatrick to shut down the state bank in 1843 without repaying people who had placed their money in it. Many wealthy farmers and businesspeople were suddenly left penniless. Then, an epidemic of yellow fever (a viral disease transmitted by infected mosquitoes) killed hundreds of people across Alabama.

No one in Alabama suffered more during this period than did the slaves. By the 1850s almost half of Alabama's population was enslaved. The majority of the slaves worked on plantations and small farms where, from sunrise to sunset, they picked cotton by hand. It was backbreaking labor, leaving the men, women, and children who worked the fields with aching bodies and bleeding fingers at the end of each day.

MOBILE BAY

In the nineteenth century cotton was king in Alabama. Much of this cotton left the state at Mobile, from which it was shipped to other states and countries. In 1861, the year the Civil War began, slaves and Irishmen loaded a million bales of cotton onto ships in Mobile Bay. This variation of a sailor's song was created by them.

pump a - way.   John - ny come tell us and pump a - way.   pump a - way.

And how many bales can you carry on?
Johnny come tell us and pump away.
Just hurry up before she's gone.
Johnny come tell us and pump away. *Chorus*

The times are hard and the wages low,
Johnny come tell us and pump away.
Just one more bale before we go,
Johnny come tell us and pump away. *Chorus*

If ever good luck does come my way,
Johnny come tell us and pump away.
I'll say goodbye to Mobile Bay,
Johnny come tell us and pump away. *Chorus*

As the nineteenth century progressed, more and more Northerners began to condemn the practice of slavery. They wanted to outlaw slavery throughout the nation. The Alabama Platform, adopted by the Democratic State Convention of 1848, argued that each state had the right to determine whether its citizens could own slaves. In the years that followed, the arguments between Northerners and Southerners over the issues of slavery and states' rights became ever louder.

At the Democratic National Convention of 1860 Alabamian William Lowndes Yancey campaigned for the passage of the Alabama Platform. Yancey claimed that anyone who did not agree with this platform was not a Democrat. Yancey therefore proposed that any Alabamian candidate who did not go along with this platform would not be supported by the states' Democrats. When the Democratic convention refused to adopt the Alabama Platform, Yancey led the entire state delegation back to Alabama and out of the national Democratic Party. The refusal of Alabama and other Southern states to support the Democratic candidate in the presidential election of 1860 was a major factor in the election of the Republican Abraham Lincoln. The new president supported a strong federal government and opposed slavery.

Alabama native William Lowndes Yancey supported the Alabama Platform's passage at the Democratic National Convention of 1860.

On January 11, 1861, Alabama officially seceded from the Union, declaring itself the independent Republic of Alabama. Less than a month later, Alabama joined with its Southern neighbors to form the Confederate States of America. Montgomery was chosen as the Confederacy's first capital.

Vowing to preserve the Union at all costs, President Lincoln sent Union soldiers to ports along the Southern shores. On April 12, 1861, the Civil War began. The most important battle fought in Alabama took place in Mobile Bay in 1864, when Union admiral David G. Farragut was said to have soundly defeated the Confederate forces. By the end of the Civil War, in 1865, the Confederacy finally surrendered. The war had lasted four long years, and much of the South was in ruins.

The great naval victory in Mobile Bay took place on August 5, 1864.

The years following the Civil War were not easy ones in Alabama. The state legislature, for instance, refused to ratify the Fourteenth Amendment to the Constitution of the United States—the amendment that provided civil rights to all African Americans. Because of this refusal, President Andrew Johnson placed Alabama under military rule, a move that angered may Alabamians. Then pro-Union Alabamians (mostly from northern Alabama) and many blacks came together to form a state Republican party, which eventually took over Alabama's state government. Under the Republican Party's rule, the state was readmitted to the Union in 1868.

As the economy began to improve, cities such as Birmingham grew more stable. The Freemen's Bureau, a federal government agency, helped to supply much-needed food to the freed slaves and other portions of the state's population that were suffering from widespread hunger. Schools for freed slaves were established by the Freemen's Bureau, as were standards to regulate the wages paid to them. During the time of Republican rule in Alabama, from 1867 to 1874, African Americans, such as Benjamin Turner, Jeremiah Haralson, and James T. Rapier, were elected to the U.S. Congress.

But there were still many problems in Alabama. A group called the Ku Klux Klan, invigorated by its popularity, used violence to force blacks and Republican whites to stay away from the voting booths. As a result, the formerly pro-Confederate whites who made up much of the Democratic Party at that time, especially in southern Alabama, took back the leadership of the state government in the election of 1874.

While the Republicans spent a lot of money on the reconstruction of the state, including the construction of new railroads and other forms of transportation, charges of corruption and wasted funds were loudly made against them by their opponents. When the Democrats came back into power, government spending was cut, which resulted in a widespread lack of support for education. Another problem many Alabamians faced was the abolition of sharecropping. Powerful landowners controlled the land, but after the abolition of slavery, they had no one to work their fields and little money to pay wages. Freed slaves, on the other hand, had farming skills but no land and no jobs. Through sharecropping the landowners leased their land and provided seeds and farm implements, while the share-

Sharecroppers farmed Alabama's soil, turning over half their crop to the landowner.

croppers did the work. Sharecroppers (both black and white) were supposed to receive half the harvest in return, but accounts of abuse of this system were extensive. Landowners charged high interest on loans and kept shoddy bookkeeping records that worked out in their favor. Sharecropping began to look like little more than legalized slavery.

Mining and iron production blossomed in the central and northern parts of the state. Hundreds of mines sprung up in northern Alabama, unearthing the region's iron and charcoal. Soon, Birmingham became one of the world's great iron and steel centers. Alabama may not have held the gold that Hernando de Soto had searched for, but the state was home to an abundance of other metals.

THE LEGEND OF HENRY WELLS

On a stormy night in the small town of Carrollton, children crowded nervously around the courthouse to catch a glimpse of one of Alabama's strangest attractions. According to local legend, the image of the former slave Henry Wells appears momentarily on one of the courthouse's second-story windows each time a lightning bolt fills the night sky with light.

As the story goes, a raging fire destroyed Carrollton's original courthouse in 1876. Wells was suspected of setting the fire, but he escaped the area. Two years later Wells was arrested in another part of the state and brought back to Carrollton for his trial. As the news spread that Wells had been captured, an angry crowd gathered outside the recently rebuilt courthouse.

In the decades following the Civil War African Americans accused of serious crimes were often lynched, or hanged without a trial. To protect Wells from the mob, authorities secretly moved him to a guarded room on the second floor. While a powerful thunderstorm settled over the area, Wells watched the angry crowd with terror, his face pressed against the second-story windowpane. All at once a bolt of lightning crashed down on the street below, momentarily scattering the crowd. According to legend the sudden burst of bright light permanently engraved Wells's image on the window. Wells was later killed while attempting to escape, but his story remains a vital legend in Carrollton.

Alabama suffered a number of setbacks during the early twentieth century. During the early decades a tiny insect called the boll weevil invaded the state's cotton fields by the billions. Entire crops were quickly destroyed. Many farmers were left in financial ruin. During the same period the Great Depression swept across the nation and the world. Between 1929 and 1931 most banks in Alabama were forced to close, leaving depositors without their money. Tens of thousands of Alabamians lost their jobs, as the steel mills and coal mines also shut down. Cotton prices fell to five cents a pound, so it was hardly worth picking it.

Alabama's future brightened when the federal government created several different programs in the state. One of the most important was the Tennessee Valley Authority (TVA), which was established in 1933. Through this program, cheap electric power was generated through the creation of two dams on the Tennessee River in Alabama. This project created jobs. Then, with the inexpensive electricity supplied by these new plants, the state's iron and steel factories slowly recovered and thus provided even more jobs for thousands of the state's unemployed. The TVA also provided jobs in the replanting of trees in Alabama's forests. In addition, this program invested in agricultural research, especially in the development and use of fertilizers to improve plant production.

Other federal programs included the building of military bases, especially in southern Alabama. When World War II broke out, the money poured into these bases stimulated the state's economy further. As a result, Mobile became home to a large shipbuilding industry, and Birmingham's steel production flourished.

TUSKEGEE

In the late nineteenth century an educator named Booker T. Washington was responsible for one of the most significant events in Alabama history. The son of an Virginia enslaved family, Washington used money he received from foundations and philanthropists to establish the Tuskegee Normal and Industrial Institute, founded in 1881 in the small town of Tuskegee, Alabama. Washington believed that education was the key to the liberation of black people in the United States. Students at the school worked the farmland around Tuskegee while studying agricultural sciences and other subjects. Washington eventually transformed the small, experimental school into the nation's most respected educational institution for blacks.

In 1896 Washington hired a brilliant young African-American scientist named George Washington Carver to teach at the institute. Carver was already respected for his research in botany, the study of plants, and mycology, the study of mushrooms and other fungi. During the decades he taught at Tuskegee, Carver became one of the world's leading botanists and one of the nation's leading educators. His specialty was finding creative uses for common plants and vegetables. His most famous innovations involved the peanuts that grew in abundance in the rich Black Belt soil around Tuskegee. Over the years Carver and his students created 325 products from the peanut.

Another federal program, the Work Projects Administration, gave jobs to Alabama's unemployed writers, commissioning them to record the oral histories of the people of the state.

THE CIVIL RIGHTS MOVEMENT

But Alabama's renewed prosperity did not reach everyone. The nearly one million African Americans who lived there continued to suffer under the Jim Crow laws, which had existed since the decades following the Civil War. Under this system of racial segregation, or separation, black Alabamians were not allowed to enroll in the same schools, hold the same positions, or use the same water fountains, bathrooms, or other public facilities as white Alabamians. This began to change in 1954, when the U.S. Supreme Court declared racial segregation in public schools to be unconstitutional. Inspired by the Court's historic decision, many African Americans in Alabama began to struggle openly for their rights.

Things heated up the following year, when a woman in Montgomery named Rosa Parks refused to surrender her bus seat to a white man. At the time, blacks in Alabama and throughout the South were required by law to sit in the back of public buses. If the whites-only section became full, black riders had to give up their seats in the back of the bus to white riders.

Parks had always felt that segregated seating was unfair. She had often tried to take a seat closer to the front of the bus, but each time she failed. On several occasions drivers had asked her to leave the bus. "Our treatment was just not right," Parks would later say, "and I was tired of it. I kept thinking about my mother and my grandparents, and how strong they were. I knew there was a possibility of being mistreated, but an opportunity was being given to me to do what I had asked of others."

POPULATION GROWTH: 1800–2000

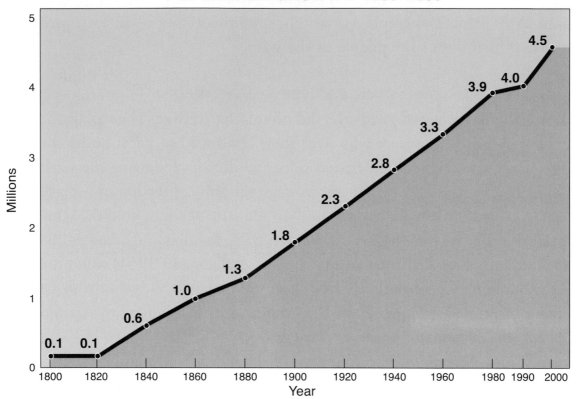

When Parks refused to leave the bus, she was arrested and brought to trial for breaking Montgomery's racial-segregation laws. Outraged by her treatment, Martin Luther King Jr., a local minister at Dexter Avenue Baptist Church, and other activists, such as E. D. Nixon, organized a boycott of the Montgomery bus system. To protest Parks's arrest, African Americans began walking and carpooling to and from work each day instead of riding the bus. Since nearly half of Montgomery's citizens were African American, the boycott, which lasted for more than a year, devastated the city's transportation system. In November 1956 the U.S. Supreme Court finally ruled on

Rosa Parks is fingerprinted in Montgomery in 1956 after her arrest for organizing a boy-cott of the city's buses.

Parks's case by declaring that segregated seating in public transportation was unconstitutional.

But this did not end the public conflict over civil rights in Alabama. A key figure in this conflict was George Corley Wallace, who would soon become Alabama's outspoken governor. In 1958 Wallace began his campaign for governor as a progressive Democrat who supported greater rights for blacks and other poor Alabamians. After he was soundly defeated by a racist white candidate, Wallace changed his stance on racial issues. With his new platform as a vocal supporter of segregation, Wallace was elected to four terms as governor during the next three decades.

In 1963 Wallace brought international attention to the state once again when he stood defiantly at the doorway of Foster Auditorium at the University of Alabama and refused to allow black students to enroll at the school. In response, President John F. Kennedy sent in the National Guard, and the students were eventually allowed to attend. However, Wallace's bold stance made him the spokesperson for white people who supported segregation. Wallace ran for president as an independent candidate in 1968 and

Governor George Wallace (far left) stands in a doorway at the University of Alabama to prevent the desegregation of the school.

then in 1972 and 1976 as a Democrat. Though he was not elected, he received millions of votes across the country.

CONTINUING THE STRUGGLE INTO THE TWENTY-FIRST CENTURY

Over the years since the Civil Rights Act of 1964 was passed, black and white Alabamians have worked together to improve their state and to protect the rights of all its citizens. Surprisingly, a leader in the state's efforts was George Wallace himself. During his final campaign for governor, in 1982, Wallace completely changed his position on racial issues yet again, speaking out on behalf of the rights and needs of the state's black citizens. Wallace focused Alabama politics on such issues as health care, public education, and the creation of new jobs that would benefit all the state's citizens.

Birmingham's population in 2007 was 73 percent black. What has happened in Birmingham is typical of what is occurring in other cities in the United States. It is called "white flight," a tendency for white people to move to the suburbs, while many black people remain in the city. Birmingham, like other cities in Alabama, is working to solve this new form of segregation by enticing people from all backgrounds to move back to the city in order to help develop trust among a more varied population. As quoted in a 2007 news article in the *Birmingham News*, Ed LaMonte, a political science professor at Birmingham-Southern College and former director of the Center for Urban Affairs at the University of Alabama at Birmingham, pointed out, "If we are to move ahead, we need vision, leadership and trust."

Racial issues are not the only challenges Alabama is facing in the twenty-first century. Much of the South, including Alabama, has been suffering from a severe drought, which impacts Alabama's agriculture and also creates the potential for massive wildfires. But on the upside, Alabama's economy is improving, and unemployment figures hit a record low in October 2007. New businesses, such as a German-based steel manufacturer that has invested in plant construction in Mobile County, are creating new jobs. Environmental awareness is also thriving. Alabama's state government, conscious of global warming, is supporting the use of cleaner-burning fuel by setting up gas stations along Alabama's major highways to make alternative fuels available to the general public.

The twenty-first century will bring a mix of tough challenges that Alabamians will have to deal with. But with the improving economy, the drive to protect the environment, and the emphasis placed on developing and enriching the state's education system, Alabamians are working together to keep their state a thriving environment.

Chapter Three

The Heart of Dixie

With Tennessee to the north, Georgia to the east, Mississippi to the west, and Florida to the south, Alabama is the geographical center of the Deep South. In the 1950s the state's chamber of commerce dreamed up the slogan "The Heart of Dixie" to make Alabama stand out. Alabamians came to like the distinction, and in 1955 this slogan was printed on Alabama license plates. The slogan and the distinction of being the heart of Dixie stuck for a while, but now the plates say "Stars Fell on Alabama."

BLACK AND WHITE

For most people in Alabama, being southern means sharing a common history and a common way of life. But while the lives of most black and white Alabamians have been shaped by the same past and the same dramatic events, the groups have very different memories of their shared history.

In recent years one issue dividing black and white residents has been the continued use of the Confederate battle flag across the state. Many white Alabamians still choose to demonstrate their southern pride by displaying

Schoolchildren celebrate American-Indian culture at the Moundville Archaeological Park.

this Confederate flag on T-shirts, caps, and bumper stickers or draped across the rear windows of pickup trucks.

For many black Alabamians, however, the display of the Confederate battle flag is a sore spot. "It's just so insensitive to keep using it," complains a store owner in Mobile, "and you still see it everywhere you go. I know that lots of people don't mean any harm by it, but to me, that flag represents a time and a way of life when my ancestors were slaves. So of course it upsets me every time I see it."

The Confederate flag flew over Alabama's capitol until 1993. Since then, there have been demonstrations held in front of the capitol in which protestors demanded that the Confederate flag be reinstated. So far the flag has not returned, though presidential candidates touring the state are often asked a question about it as a way to evaluate their position on this issue.

Demonstrators rally at the capitol in Montgomery in an effort to have the Confederate flag flown over the building.

ETHNIC ALABAMA

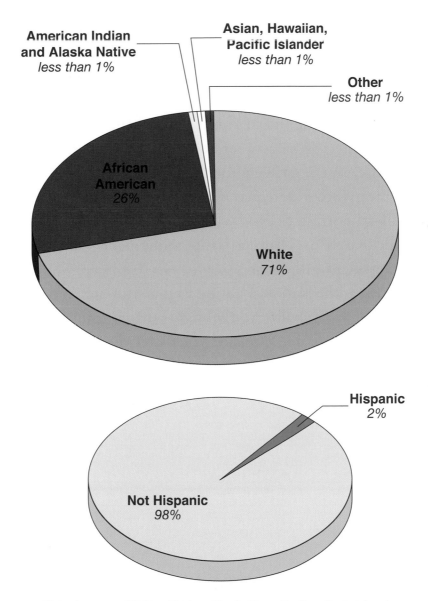

American Indian and Alaska Native
less than 1%

Asian, Hawaiian, Pacific Islander
less than 1%

Other
less than 1%

African American
26%

White
71%

Hispanic
2%

Not Hispanic
98%

Note: A person of Cuban, Mexican, Puerto Rican, South or Central American, or other Spanish culture or origin, regardless of race, is defined as Hispanic.

Today, in spite of their differences, black and white Alabamians are increasingly finding ways to share the memories and symbols of their state's past. Throughout the state thousands of black and white citizens visit memorials to the two most dramatic and significant events in the state's troubled history: the Civil War and the civil rights movement.

Visitors to Selma can learn about both of these events. Each April actors re-create the 1865 Battle of Selma, the state's only major inland Civil War battle. In the struggle for the Confederate army's largest iron foundry, Union forces defeated Confederate troops led by General Nathan Bedford Forrest. Forrest would later become famous as the first leader of the Ku Klux Klan, a white supremacist organization that became powerful after the war.

Across town at the National Voting Rights Museum and Institute, the same visitors can learn about the civil rights march from Selma to Montgomery that took place one hundred years after the Battle of Selma.

THE POARCH BAND OF THE CREEK NATION

With the unusual distinction of never having been removed from their land, the Poarch people have lived outside of Atmore (northeast of Mobile) for more than three hundred years. This band of Creek Indians is the only federally recognized group of American Indians left in Alabama. The Poarch are a sovereign nation, which means that they have their own government and bylaws. About 2,300 people belong to this nation, with about 1,000 of them living on the Poarch Reservation.

People of different cultures are slowly beginning to cross boundaries in Alabama.

According to an article in the *Birmingham News*, remedying "white flight" takes time and trust. Erica Young is quoted as stating, "Each community, even though it's part of the larger Birmingham metro area, is so isolated." And this can lead to problems. People from the suburbs are afraid to go into the city, and people in the city are afraid to travel to the suburbs. People get used to spending their whole days, their whole lives, in the isolated communities in which they live. They shop, go to school, and entertain themselves among people who have the same skin color. There is no social intermingling and therefore no building of trust among the different cultures that make up Alabama's population. Things are changing, this same article points out, but it will take a lot of time.

Alabama lies near the center of the region known as the Bible Belt. Baptists account for more than half of the state's churchgoers. Methodists, making up a little more than 10 percent, are the next largest group, followed by Roman Catholics, at slightly more than 4 percent.

Each Sunday morning the state's roads are heavy with traffic as families drive to their local churches. In hundreds of small towns throughout the state the steeples and spires that rise above the churches are often the tallest sights on the horizon.

Alabamians are typically very proud of—and very vocal about—their religious beliefs. Many believe that it is extremely important to share their religious beliefs and values with other people.

Throughout the state's history, Alabamians have frequently taken public positions based on their religious beliefs. In the 1950s Martin Luther King Jr. used his pulpit at Dexter Avenue Baptist Church to condemn the racial segregation that was practiced at the time. In recent years Protestants in Alabama have spoken out in support of a number of causes, often involving the rights of citizens to express their religious beliefs in public settings, such as public schools and workplaces. Other issues have also emerged, such as the attempt by religious groups to abolish Alabama's capital punishment—the putting to death of criminals convicted of serious offenses.

Churchgoers at the Dexter Avenue Baptist Church in Montgomery.

JUDGE ROY MOORE AND THE TEN COMMANDMANTS

A 2003 case involved Chief Justice Roy Moore's insistence on keeping a Ten Commandments monument he had installed inside the State Supreme Court building. A federal court had ruled that, as a public servant, the judge did not have the right to express his private religious beliefs in the courtroom. The court's ruling was based on "the separation of church and state," a legal doctrine that ensures that both the government and religious institutions can operate independent of one another's control. Conservative Christians, including the governor, rallied in Montgomery to express their dissatisfaction with the State Supreme Court's decision. In 1998 Judge Moore and his supporters won a temporary victory when the State Supreme Court dismissed the case, thereby avoiding making a ruling. But in 2003 Judge Moore was removed from office when his own Alabama colleagues ruled against him.

SPORTS

Sports play an enormous role in the lives of Alabamians. Everywhere you go in the state, there are signs of some type of sporting event—from sprawling green golf courses and soccer fields to huge football stadiums and speedways in Talladega, Birmingham, and countless other places across the state.

However, when most people in Alabama talk about sports, the first thing they mention is football—especially the fierce rivalry between the state's two powerhouses, the University of Alabama (affectionately called Bama by its fans) and Auburn University. From the waterways of northwest Alabama to the sandy shores of the Gulf, virtually everyone in the state has something to say about the rivalry. "Sports are almost like a religion here in Alabama," confides a student at Auburn, "especially football. Sometimes things get a little crazy in the fall, especially when it comes to the Auburn-Alabama rivalry. I've actually seen family members who wouldn't even speak to each other during the weekend of the game, because each one was rooting for a different team. During the football season, just about everybody in the state is either an Alabama fan or an Auburn fan. It's just not something you can be neutral about."

Auburn University fans celebrate after defeating the University of Florida.

With their record over the years, the two teams have certainly given Alabamians plenty to talk about. The University of Alabama, one of the most successful teams in the history of college football, had won twelve national titles as of fall 2007. Some of the game's most talented and popular athletes—including quarterbacks Bart Starr and Joe Namath—first received national attention while playing at Alabama.

But it was the team's legendary coach, Paul "Bear" Bryant, who captured the imagination and respect of the people of Alabama. Bryant led the University of Alabama to six national championships and became the most successful coach in college football history, with 323 wins overall. Even Alabama's rivals at Auburn were in awe of Bryant's accomplishments and respectful of his memory.

In recent years, however, Auburn has begun to challenge Alabama's dominance as the state's best team. During the 1970s and 1980s two of the team's outstanding players—quarterback Pat Sullivan and running back Bo Jackson—received the Heisman Trophy as the best college football player. Between 2000 and 2006 Auburn has defeated Bama in the Iron Bowl, their traditional football game at the end of the season, five out of six times.

The second most popular sport in Alabama is NASCAR stock-car racing. Located east of Birmingham, the Talladega Superspeedway hosts some of the world's fastest stock cars. The shelves and bedsides of youngsters throughout the state support model race cars and photographs of top drivers. Each October racing fans from around the country crowd into the speedway to watch the Winston 500. "For my money and my time," says an automobile mechanic in Auburn, "there's nothing in this world that's more exciting than car racing. You've got the speed and the roar of the tires and all that energy among the crowd. There's just absolutely nowhere I'd rather be than up there at Talladega. Nowhere."

Stock cars fight for position at the Talladega Superspeedway.

Another newer development in sports is the game of golf. In the late 1980s Dr. David Bronner, CEO of the Retirement Systems of Alabama, wanted to find a way to increase the assets of the state's pension fund. Bronner also thought Alabama's tourism industry could use a boost. So, he came up with an idea that would do both. He promoted the development of a series of eight spectacular golf courses throughout the state. He wanted these golf courses to be some of the best in the world, so he enlisted the help of the world-renowned golf course designer Robert Trent Jones Sr. Later, in 2005, two more courses were added to the series, which is called the Robert Trent Jones

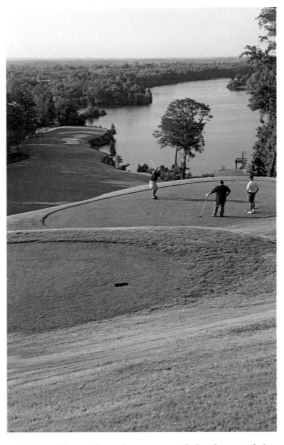

Avid golfers take advantage of the beautiful course at the Robert Trent Jones Golf Trail in Prattville.

Golf Trail. Bronner's plan worked. Today, the trail attracts golfers from all over the United States as well as from other countries, making Alabama one of the most popular golfing destinations in the world. An estimated 500,000 golfers now use the trail. The pension program is also doing well and is investing in high-class hotels along the courses to house the many visitors.

SAUSAGE, CHEESE, AND GRITS CASSEROLE

In Alabama and throughout the South grits (the popular name for ground hominy corn) are both a favorite breakfast food and a key ingredient in many dinner casseroles. Have an adult help you with this recipe.

6 cups water

11/2 cups quick-cooking grits

2 tablespoons unsalted butter

2 large pickled jalapeño pepper, finely minced

4 scallions, finely chopped

21/2 cups cheddar or Monterey Jack cheese, shredded

3/4 pound fresh sausage, casings removed

1 tablespoon vegetable oil

1 onion, finely chopped

1 large red or green bell pepper, finely chopped

4 large eggs

2 teaspoons hot sauce

Salt and pepper to taste

Preheat oven to 350 degrees Fahrenheit. In a large saucepan, bring the water to a boil and slowly stir in the grits. Cover and simmer, stirring occasionally, for 7 minutes. Stir in the butter, minced jalapeño, chopped scallions, and 11/2 cups of the cheese. Add salt and pepper to taste. Stir until the cheese is melted, and then spread the mixture in a buttered 9 x 13-inch baking dish.

Brown the sausage over medium heat in a heavy skillet, stirring frequently and breaking up the lumps. Use a slotted spoon to transfer the sausage to a paper towel. Drain the fat from the skillet, and then add the vegetable oil. Cook the chopped onion and bell pepper over medium heat, stirring occasionally until both are soft. Whisk together the eggs and hot sauce in a large bowl, adding salt to taste. Stir in the sausage and the onions and peppers, and then spread the entire mixture over the grits. Sprinkle the remaining cheese over the top.

Bake until the eggs are firm, about 30 minutes. Serve hot.

In 2007 Alabama had an estimated population of 4,627,851. Of this number, about 71 percent were white, 26 percent were black, and the remaining 3 percent included Hispanic, Asian, and American-Indian people. The greatest density of people is found in the metropolitan areas, with Birmingham the largest. According to a 2006 estimated count, Birmingham's population had decreased by several thousand in the previous few years but still contained about 229,424 people. The largest ethnic

Birmingham is the most populous city in Alabama and is home to the greatest number of African Americans in the state.

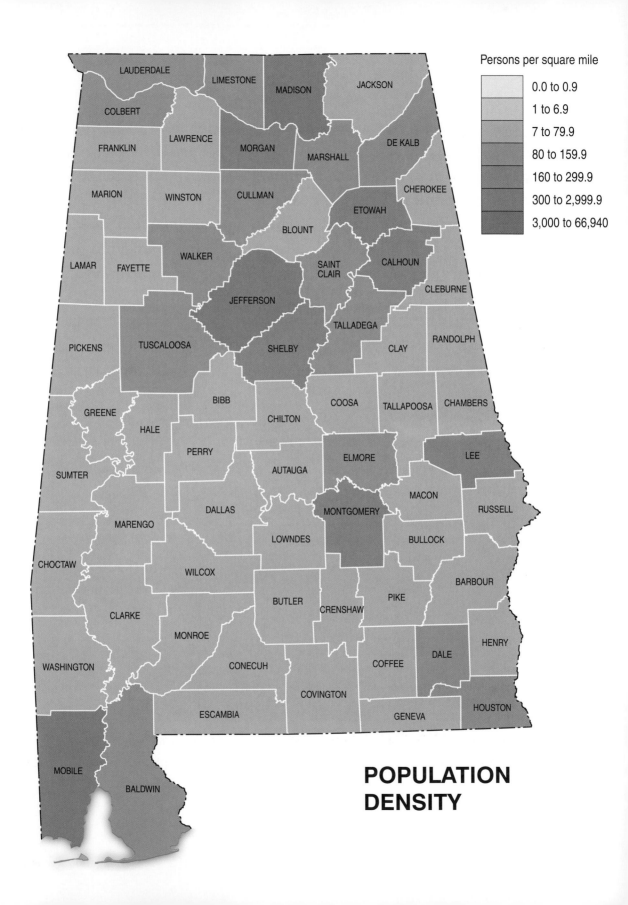

Persons per square mile

0.0 to 0.9
1 to 6.9
7 to 79.9
80 to 159.9
160 to 299.9
300 to 2,999.9
3,000 to 66,940

POPULATION DENSITY

group in Birmingham is African American, at around 70 percent; 4 percent of this group was born in Africa. The total population is rather young, with about 36 percent under the age of twenty-four. Those claiming white ancestry mostly have roots in the European countries of England, Germany, Ireland, Scotland, and France.

Montgomery, the capital of Alabama, ranks second in population, with a 2006 estimate of 201,998. Montgomery's black to white ratio is more balanced than Birmingham's, with both groups hovering around 50 percent. Small proportions of the city's population are made up of American Indians, Asian Americans, and Hispanics, who are the largest of the three minority groups, at a little more than 1 percent. Montgomery is proud of its Civil War and civil rights museums. However, the city also houses the fifth largest fine arts museum in the world.

Mobile is Alabama's third largest city, with a 2006 estimated population of 192,830. Mobile is more than three hundred years old. At first it was the capital of the French Louisiana Territory, and the French influence—including its own Mardi Gras celebration—remains evident. Mobile also offers the only deepwater port in the state. The black and white populations are equal in size in Mobile. The Hispanic and Asian populations are also balanced, at around 1.7 percent each. Mobile is home to Spring Hill College, the first Catholic college in the southeastern United States, the third oldest Jesuit college in the country, and the oldest four-year college in Alabama. It is also home to the state's newest public university, the University of South Alabama, chartered in 1963.

Of the four largest cities in Alabama, Huntsville is the least populous, with a 2006 estimate of about 168,132. Huntsville is located in northern Alabama and is famous for its space research station, the George C. Marshall Space Flight Center. Huntsville also has the largest space museum in the

STEADY INCREASE IN HISPANIC POPULATION

In some Alabama counties the enrollment of Hispanic children in schools increased by 12 percent from 2006 to 2007. Expectations are that this trend will continue. In communities that have jobs to offer, an editorial in the *Birmingham News* noted, the number of Hispanics is likely to increase. The official 2000 U.S. Census figures stated that there were about 76,000 Hispanics in Alabama.

People who work with immigrants (such as medical clinic workers, social workers, and those involved with churches) have stated that the actual number could well be twice that. The Hispanic population is spread all over the state, both in urban and rural settings. The highest populations are in metropolitan Birmingham. Immigrants play a significant role in many of Alabama's industries—in the agricultural and timber businesses as well in the urban tourism business.

world, the U.S. Space and Rocket Center. The majority of the population is white, at over 63 percent; with blacks making up 30 percent. Other groups include Asian Indian, Chinese, and Hispanic people.

Alabama is made up of people from all over the world who share differences as well as similarities and who are willing to reach out and learn from each other as they make this state their home.

A visitor enjoys his time at Huntsville's U.S. Space and Rocket Center.

Chapter Four

The Laws of the State

Each state has its own form of government and its own style of making and changing laws. This is why each state has its own constitution. Alabama's current state constitution was adopted in 1901. Today, that constitution is causing a lot of controversy in Alabama. For the past several decades a battle between those who think the constitution is outdated and those who think making changes to the constitution will harm Alabamians has been raging. There is no clear information about which side will win. Like governmental issues of the past, Alabamians seem to take their time in making changes. Until a change is made, the present state constitution remains the basis for how the government functions.

INSIDE GOVERNMENT

Alabama's government is divided into three branches: executive, legislative, and judicial.

Executive

The chief executive of Alabama is the governor. He or she prepares the state budget and develops policies in areas ranging from education to economic

Alabama's capitol is a National Historic Landmark. Jefferson Davis was inaugurated as president of the Confederate States there, and Martin Luther King Jr. gave a moving speech there at the end of the Selma-to-Montgomery civil rights march.

Alabama governor Bob Riley speaks about the sales tax holiday that took place in 2006.

development. The governor, who is elected every four years, many serve no more than two consecutive terms. The same is true for the lieutenant governor, who takes over if the governor must leave office during the term.

Other executive branch officials include the attorney general, the state auditor, the secretary of state, the state treasurer, and the commissioner of agriculture and industries.

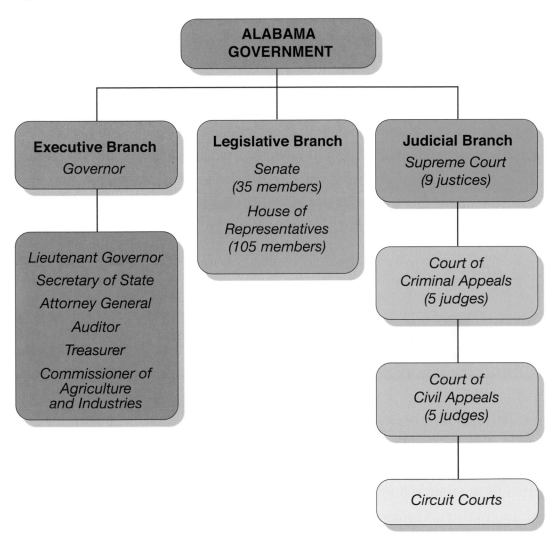

Legislative

The Alabama legislature consists of a senate with 35 members and a house of representatives with 105 members. All legislators are elected to four-year terms. The legislature is responsible for approving budgets and drafting and approving new legislation. After the legislature approves a proposed law, called a bill, it is sent to the governor to be signed. If the governor signs the bill, it becomes a law. If the governor vetoes, or rejects, the bill, it can still become law if it is passed by a majority of members in both the senate and the house.

Judicial

Alabama's highest court is the State Supreme Court. It is composed of a chief justice and eight associate judges, who are elected to six-year terms.

Most of Alabama's criminal and civil trials are heard in the circuit courts. If someone challenges a decision made in a circuit court, the case is heard either by the court of criminal appeals or the court of civil appeals, each of which has five judges. If the ruling of the appellate court is also challenged, the case is then sent to the State Supreme Court for a hearing.

EDUCATION

Historically, many Alabamians have suffered from poor education. The Alabama legislature did not create a statewide public education system until 1854, thirty-five years after statehood was granted. Even after public schools were established, poor children worked in the fields for most of the year. The children of slaves received no schooling at all.

After slavery was abolished, black children and white children were educated in separate schools, and far more money was spent on the schools for white children. Consequently, black children received a poorer education.

THE HARD ROAD TO CHANGE

One of the big questions facing Alabamians in the past few decades has been whether to change the century-old state constitution, one of the oldest state constitutions in the nation. Some argue that the constitution is too long (it currently contains almost eight hundred amendments) and that it contains a failed tax structure and strips many of the state's citizens (especially the poor and marginalized minorities) of power. One critic of the current constitution, Dr. Joe A. Sumners, has stated that Alabama is the only southern state to deny the state's counties local home rule. In other words, all local issues are handled in Montgomery, thus disallowing "local governments from addressing local problems." Revising the state constitution could remedy this, according to Dr. Sumners. Many proponents for change believe both social and economic progress is thwarted by the old constitution. Over the decades several governors, as far back as Emmet O'Neal in 1915, Thomas Kilby in the 1920s, Jim Folsom in the 1940s, and Albert Brewer in the 1960s, have tried to bring about constitutional reform but have failed to do so.

A state constitution can be changed in two ways: through amendments or through rewriting during a constitutional convention. Since many people find that Alabama's current number of amendments is too large, it makes the constitution too complicated. Adding more amendments is not a very satisfactory solution. The legislature must pass a bill in order for a constitutional convention to be held, and the public must vote its approval. Delegates to the convention would then rewrite the constitution, and again a public vote would be needed to ratify it.

Those against reforming the state constitution fear that taxes would dramatically increase and that references to God would be removed from it. Providing home rule to local counties is also a concern of some people, who prefer the centralized power of the state legislature.

**ALABAMA
BY COUNTY**

Not until after schools began to be desegregated in the 1960s did equal education become available to black children.

In the 1980s Governor George Wallace began pushing to improve education. He helped pass a $310 million statewide bond that has been responsible for dramatic improvements in the quality of Alabama's public schools. Since then Alabama has made education a priority. One important step has been to adopt strict standards for core courses. Public high school students must now complete four years of English, social studies, science, and mathematics.

In 2008 Governor Bob Riley published his plan for Alabama schools. Included in his goals is greater availability of the ACCESS Distance Learning Program, which, at the beginning of 2008, provided more than 170 schools with a wider variety of courses taught via the Internet. Money for new school construction and an expansion of the Advanced Placement course program in math, science, English, and social studies were also planned.

Educating Alabama's children is one of the top priorities of the current administration.

Chapter Five

Making a Living

During Alabama's early history its economy was built around farming—principally cotton—and textile production. For more than a century most Alabamians, both black and white, made their living in the cotton fields or working in some part of the cotton textile industry. But after the boll weevil destroyed thousands of acres of cotton in the early twentieth century, people began to look for more reliable ways to make a living.

WORKING ON ALABAMA'S FARMS

As of 2002 Alabama had 8.9 million acres of farmland, which represented a little more than 27 percent of the total land in the state. Estimated 2006 figures listed that there were 43,000 farms in Alabama. Of that farmland, almost 4 million acres were listed as cropland, a decrease of almost 250,000 acres from the previous decade. Most of Alabama's farms are relatively small, averaging only about 200 acres apiece. Three-fourths of Alabama's farmlands are devoted to raising livestock, such as chickens and cattle. In 2004 Alabama ranked third in the nation in the production of broiler chickens. The remaining one-fourth

Many commercial fishing boats are built in Bayou La Batre. The industry employs between seven hundred and one thousand workers. This worker is welding the bottom of a ship.

Many of Alabama's farmers raise livestock.

of farmland is devoted to growing crops, including cotton, hay, soybeans, and such vegetables as potatoes and corn. Peanuts are also grown in abundance in the wiregrass region. The most important farm products are poultry, cotton, peanuts, feed crops, and wheat.

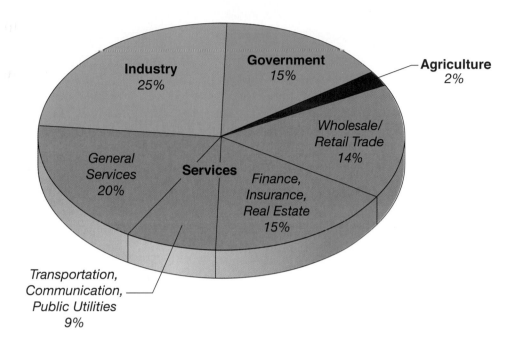

2006 GROSS STATE PRODUCT: $160 Million

Industry
25%

Government
15%

Agriculture
2%

Wholesale/
Retail Trade
14%

General
Services
20%

Services

Finance,
Insurance,
Real Estate
15%

Transportation,
Communication,
Public Utilities
9%

Alabamians export billions of dollars worth of products all over the world. These include automobiles, chemicals, industrial and electrical machinery, and plastics. These goods are shipped to Europe, Asia, Canada, and South and Central America.

With more and more of Alabama's people moving out of small farming communities and into cities and towns, service industries have become increasingly important to the state's economy. They account for the biggest portion of the gross state product. These include government agencies, such as schools, insurance companies, banks, hotels and restaurants, doctors, computer software developers, transportation, utilities (like communications and electricity suppliers), and retail stores. The army and air force bases located across the state are also important to Alabama's economy.

The service industry is the largest employment sector in the state.

The George C. Marshall Space Flight Center in Huntsville, one of the most extensive research facilities of the National Aeronautics and Space Administration (NASA), is also a major employer. The Saturn V rocket that carried the first astronauts to the moon was designed and tested at the center.

The state's rich mineral supply and cheap electricity have made Alabama one of the South's centers of manufacturing. Paper, clothing, transportation equipment, and iron and steel are all produced in Alabama. Most of the state's iron and steel plants are located in Birmingham and Bessemer.

The steel manufactured in Alabama is exported to many countries around the world.

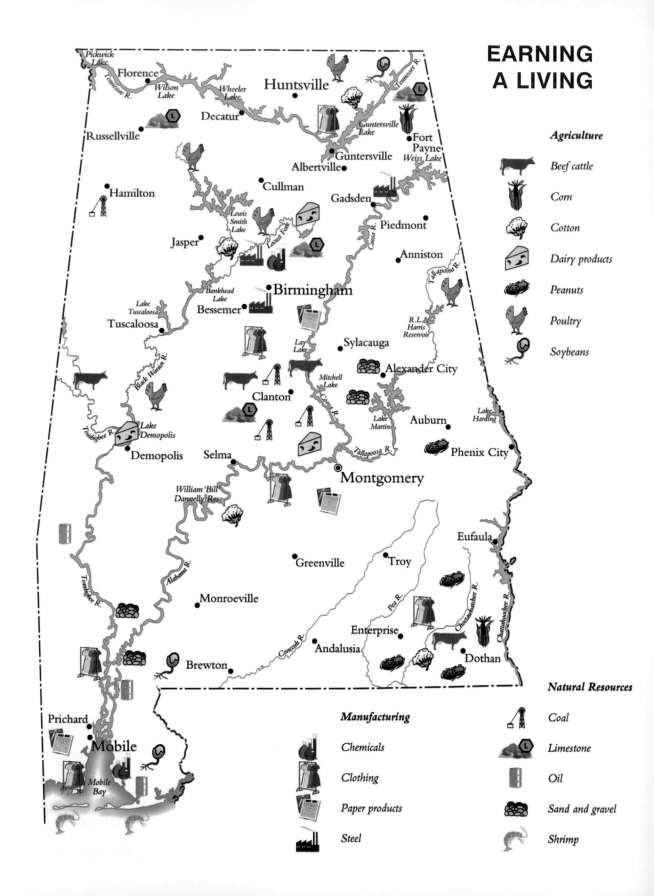

EARNING A LIVING

Agriculture

Beef cattle

Corn

Cotton

Dairy products

Peanuts

Poultry

Soybeans

Manufacturing

Chemicals

Clothing

Paper products

Steel

Natural Resources

Coal

Limestone

Oil

Sand and gravel

Shrimp

Pickwick Lake
Tennessee R.
Florence
Wilson Lake
Wheeler Lake
Huntsville
Tennessee R.
Decatur
Russellville
Guntersville Lake
Fort Payne
Hamilton
Guntersville
Albertville
Weiss Lake
Cullman
Gadsden
Lewis Smith Lake
Piedmont
Coosa R.
Jasper
Locust Fork
Anniston
Bankhead Lake
Tallapoosa R.
Birmingham
Lake Tuscaloosa
Bessemer
R.L. Harris Reservoir
Tuscaloosa
Lay Lake
Sylacauga
Black Warrior R.
Alexander City
Mitchell Lake
Clanton
Lake Harding
Coosa R.
Lake Martin
Auburn
Tombigbee R.
Lake Demopolis
Tallapoosa R.
Phenix City
Demopolis
Selma
Montgomery
William 'Bill' Dannelly Res.
Eufaula
Alabama R.
Greenville
Troy
Monroeville
Pea R.
Chattahoochee R.
Enterprise
Conecuh R.
Andalusia
Dothan
Tombigbee R.
Brewton
Prichard
Mobile
Mobile Bay

Mining is another important sector of the Alabama economy. Huge limestone quarries are scattered across the state's northeast corner, and coal mines can be found throughout north-central Alabama. Natural gas and petroleum are obtained near Mobile and in the waters of the Gulf.

Other sources of income for Alabama include forestry—primarily growing yellow pine trees—and fishing. Shrimp is the state's leading seafood, followed by blue crabs and oysters, all caught in the Gulf of Mexico. Catfish are a major freshwater fish, caught wild and also farmed in lakes and ponds across the state.

ALABAMA WORKFORCE

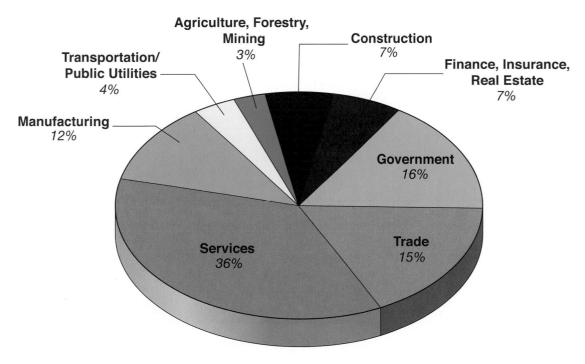

An employee at Hyundai in Montgomery works on an assembly line.

WORKING IN MANUFACTURING AND SERVICE SECTORS

In 2006 Alabama's new-job rate was higher than the national average, and the state's unemployment rate was lower than that of the United States as a whole. In 2007 Alabama's economic outlook was strong in the manufacturing sector, especially in the realm of automobile production. The service industry continued to grow, and according to journalist John Ehinger, new jobs seem to be created every week, and unemployment was at an all-time low. Searching for an economic trend, many economists point out that it depends on the region and the industry. Automobile manufacturing looks good, for instance, while the figures for the textile industry have been slumping. To stay strong, some economists have concluded, Alabama needs to invest in its education system, ensuring that students graduate from high school and go on to earn college degrees. Alabama needs to create more high-paying jobs to keep its economy healthy, and those high-paying jobs require employees with more education. Improving education was also a goal that Governor Riley expressed in an end-of-year speech in 2007. Alabamians are pulling together, studying hard, and working hard to build a stronger state.

Chapter Six

Out and About
in Alabama

From Mobile to Birmingham to Huntsville, each of Alabama's cities and towns provides a different picture of life in the state and a unique expression of Alabama's colorful history and culture.

HUNTSVILLE

Huntsville, the biggest city in northern Alabama, is known primarily as the home of the U.S. Space and Rocket Center. Along with an original Apollo rocket, which was designed in Huntsville, the museum also displays the space shuttle *Pathfinder* and a full-size Saturn V rocket.

Across town, Huntsville offers a glimpse into the past at the Alabama Constitution Village, where the state's first constitution was signed in 1819. More than a dozen buildings have been rebuilt or restored to represent the time, including a carpenter's shop and a post office. Men and women dressed in clothing from the period demonstrate how people used to make quilts, spin thread, and build furniture.

Children enjoy a day exploring the Estuarium, a public aquarium on Dauphin Island.

The U.S. Space and Rocket Center in Huntsville houses artifacts and displays from the U.S. space program.

Southeast of Huntsville is Lake Guntersville State Park, one of Alabama's most spectacular woodland areas. The park's 6,000 acres are filled with natural wonders. Bluebirds, nesting eagles, and beavers building dams are common sights, and visitors frequently stumble across the trees and shrubs in which wild turkeys roost.

THE SHOALS

West of Huntsville, the cities of Muscle Shoals, Tuscumbia, Sheffield, and Florence are scattered across both banks of the Tennessee River. To Alabamians, the entire area is known simply as the Shoals. The region's most spectacular sight is the majestic Tennessee River, along with its lakes and tributaries. "If you ask me," says a truck driver near Florence, "this is the most beautiful part of Alabama, with the big open skies and the light dancing off the river. Sometimes the sun sets so brightly on the water that I can barely see to drive."

Located near Florence, Wilson Dam has one of the world's largest single-lane water locks. The lock is a deep concrete passageway that can be filled with water to allow boats or barges to pass from one section of the river to the other. Walkways along the lock allow visitors to watch as boats slowly pass by.

The Shoals is also famous for its music. W. C. Handy, the composer known as the Father of the Blues, was born in a log cabin in Florence. The Shoals' most famous resident, Helen Keller, was born in Tuscumbia. The Keller home, Ivy Green, is preserved in its original form, including the water pump where Anne Sullivan taught Keller her first word. Each June the weeklong Helen Keller Festival features a parade through the center of Tuscumbia and several performances of *The Miracle Worker*, a play about Keller's early life.

The Tennessee River winds its way through the Shoals region of Alabama.

BIRMINGHAM

Located in north-central Alabama, Birmingham is the industrial, scientific, and cultural center of the state. It is Alabama's largest city and one of the great cities of the Deep South. In the late nineteenth century Birmingham became one of the country's leading steel producers.

THE FATHER OF THE BLUES

"Where the Tennessee River, like a silver snake, winds her way through the red clay hills of Alabama," wrote William Christopher Handy in his autobiography, "sits high on these hills my hometown, Florence. I was born in a log cabin which my grandfather had built." Today, the original log cabin in which Handy was born is preserved in Florence. A nearby museum includes the piano on which he composed many of his songs and the golden trumpet that he played on stage.

Handy first heard the blues while traveling through the Mississippi Delta in 1903. He immediately fell in love with the music. In the following years Handy began to incorporate the odd rhythms and mournful lyrics of the blues into many of his compositions, such as "The St. Louis Blues" and "The Memphis Blues." During the early decades of the twentieth century his songs brought the blues, gospel, and other African-American musical forms to an international audience for the first time.

TEN LARGEST CITIES

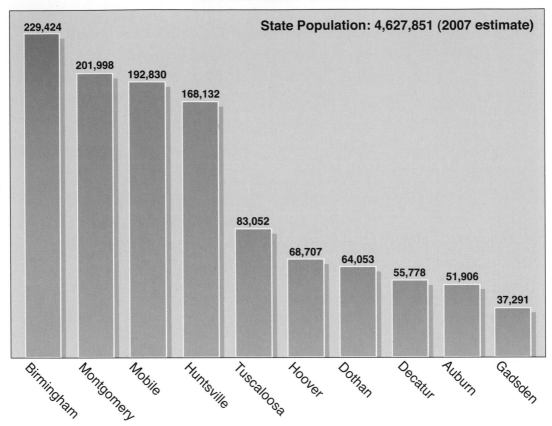

State Population: 4,627,851 (2007 estimate)

Birmingham	229,424
Montgomery	201,998
Mobile	192,830
Huntsville	168,132
Tuscaloosa	83,052
Hoover	68,707
Dothan	64,053
Decatur	55,778
Auburn	51,906
Gadsden	37,291

The city grew so fast and so much money was made there that it was nicknamed the Magic City. During the twentieth century the city's economy had expanded to include finance, education, engineering, and medical technology.

But Birmingham still bears the marks of its heyday as a city of steel. The most spectacular example of Birmingham's steel-producing past is the Sloss Furnaces National Historic Landmark. Though the furnaces shut down in 1971, the plant's massive ironworks and towering blackened smokestacks still stand and are a museum open to the public.

Another popular Birmingham site is the Alabama Sports Hall of Fame. Among its many treasures is the game ball from the University of Alabama's legendary football coach Paul "Bear" Bryant's record-breaking 315th victory and the Heisman Trophy won by Auburn University quarterback Pat Sullivan. Additional exhibits celebrate the careers of other popular Alabama sports heroes, including Willie Mays, Hank Aaron, Jesse Owens, Joe Louis, Bobby Allison, and Bart Starr.

Birmingham's most memorable sight, however, is the massive statue of the mythical god Vulcan that stands proudly atop Red Mountain in the southern part of the city. The statue was created as

Vulcan Park in Birmingham is home to the world's largest cast-iron statue.

Birmingham's contribution to the 1904 World's Fair, held in St. Louis, Missouri. Vulcan is the largest cast-iron statue in the world and the second largest statue of any type in the United States. Only the Statue of Liberty is larger. Visitors can either climb the steps or take an elevator to the top of Vulcan for a spectacular view of the city and the green, rolling hills around it.

MONTGOMERY

The state capital, Montgomery is a startling combination of the Old South and the New South. An active business center, the city has become crowded with high-rise office buildings and hotels. But at the center of the city—in the shadow of the skyscrapers—Alabama's most enduring symbols of the pre–Civil War South can be found.

The state's large white capitol stands proudly above the city's downtown on a steep green hillside called Goat Hill. Erected in 1851, the building has a massive domed center, six three-story columns guarding the entrance, and an enormous clock perched atop the roof. Inside, two magnificent circular stairways wind their way to the third floor with no visible signs of support.

LOONEY'S TAVERN

Hidden away in the heart of the Bankhead National Forest in northern Alabama's Winston County is one of the state's most interesting landmarks. A park and amphitheater mark the site of Looney's Tavern, the headquarters of pro-Union sympathizers during the Civil War.

In the years before the war most farmers in northern Alabama were relatively poor. Many of them were opposed to slavery, while others were unwilling to fight to protect a way of life that they could not afford themselves. Defying the new Confederate government, residents of the area established the "Free State of Winston," a slave-free community that continued to support the Union.

Bill Looney, popularly known as the Ol' Black Fox, led the movement from his tavern in the forest. During the Civil War he personally guided more than 2,500 people through the woods to join Union troops in Decatur and Huntsville.

The murals beneath the capitol's interior dome depict scenes from Alabama's history.

In 1861 the building served for a few months as the first capitol of the Confederate States of America. Confederate president Jefferson Davis took his oath of office on its front porch. He and his family lived briefly in the big white house that is now across from the capitol, on Washington Avenue. Today, the former presidential mansion contains an impressive collection of documents and artifacts from the Civil War period, including items that once belonged to Davis.

The Dexter Avenue King Memorial Baptist Church lies just one block from the capitol steps. In the mid-1950s Dr. Martin Luther King Jr. served as the church's pastor, gathering support for the Montgomery bus boycott from its pulpit. Today, a colorful mural in the church basement portrays the courageous people who took part in the boycott as well as other important moments in the civil rights movement.

Nearby is the Civil Rights Memorial. It was designed by the sculptor Maya Lin, who also created the Vietnam Veterans Memorial in Washington, D.C. It features a circular stone tablet bearing the names of people who sacrificed their lives for the civil rights movement. A steady stream of water washes across the surface of the stone. The wall behind the monument bears words from the Bible that King frequently quoted: "Until justice rolls down like waters and righteousness like a mighty stream."

The Civil Rights Memorial in Montgomery honors those who died during the civil rights movement.

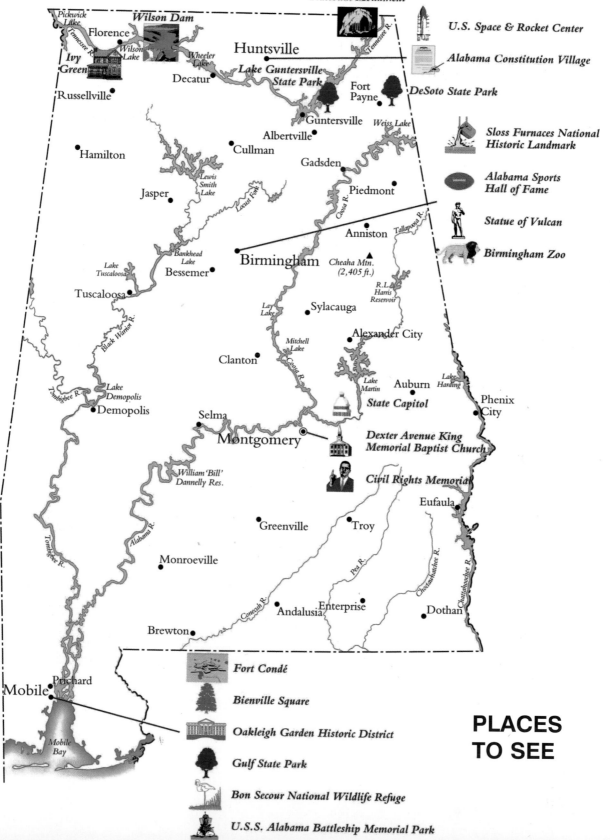

Russell Cave
National Monument

U.S. Space & Rocket Center

Alabama Constitution Village

DeSoto State Park

Sloss Furnaces National
Historic Landmark

Alabama Sports
Hall of Fame

Statue of Vulcan

Birmingham Zoo

Pickwick Lake
Ivy Green
Florence
Wilson Dam
Wilson Lake
Tennessee R.
Russellville
Decatur
Wheeler Lake
Huntsville
Tennessee R.
Hamilton
Lake Guntersville State Park
Guntersville
Albertville
Weiss Lake
Fort Payne
Cullman
Gadsden
Lewis Smith Lake
Jasper
Piedmont
Locust Fork
Coosa R.
Anniston
Tallapoosa R.
Bankhead Lake
Birmingham
Cheaha Mtn.
(2,405 ft.)
Lake Tuscaloosa
Bessemer
R.L. Harris Reservoir
Tuscaloosa
Sylacauga
Black Warrior R.
Lay Lake
Alexander City
Mitchell Lake
Lake Martin
Auburn
Lake Harding
Clanton
Coosa R.
Tombigbee R.
Lake Demopolis
Demopolis
State Capitol
Phenix City
Selma
Montgomery
Dexter Avenue King
Memorial Baptist Church
William 'Bill' Dannelly Res.
Civil Rights Memorial
Eufaula
Greenville
Troy
Alabama R.
Monroeville
Pea R.
Chattahoochee R.
Tombigbee R.
Conecuh R.
Andalusia
Enterprise
Dothan
Brewton

Fort Condé
Bienville Square
Oakleigh Garden Historic District
Prichard
Mobile
Mobile Bay
Gulf State Park
Bon Secour National Wildlife Refuge
U.S.S. Alabama Battleship Memorial Park

PLACES TO SEE

MOBILE

Mobile is Alabama's third largest city in population and its only seaport. The site of the first permanent European settlement in Alabama, it is also one of the oldest cities in the South.

At the center of the city Fort Condé, the site of the original French settlement from almost three hundred years ago, has been restored. Inside the fort's thick walls are replicas of the cannons and muskets that the French used to defend the region. In a nearby park, Bienville Square, rows and rows of giant live oak trees stand close together, their huge branches heavily draped with Spanish moss. For several weeks each spring the more than half a million azalea bushes that fill the park and line the city streets paint Mobile in dazzling crimson, white, and pink.

Oakleigh Garden Historic District features some of the Deep South's most impressive homes from the 1800s. Oakleigh, one of the largest and most beautiful of these stately mansions, was built in the 1830s and has been carefully preserved. Locals still proudly describe how President James Garfield sipped his first mint julep on the mansion's expansive front porch.

South and east of the city, Gulf State Park and the Bon Secour National Wildlife Refuge are two of the South's most popular recreational areas. The pure white sands of Gulf State Park are among the most beautiful on the Gulf Coast.

No tour of Mobile would be complete without a visit to the Oakleigh House.

MARDI GRAS IN MOBILE

While most people associate Mardi Gras with New Orleans, the festival has a longer history in Mobile. The first Mardi Gras celebration in North America was likely held in Mobile in 1703, more than seventy-five years before the event made its way to New Orleans. Mardi Gras means "fat Tuesday" in French and is the day of feasting that takes place just prior to Lent tradition-ally, a traditional time of self-sacrifice and fasting before Easter.

Today, thousands of people still line the streets to watch parades of masked revelers and colorful floats. People on the floats toss candies, coins, and other souvenirs to children in the crowd. In the Mobile version of Mardi Gras the most popular items to catch are moon pies, chocolate- or vanilla-coated graham cookies with a marshmallow center. All along the parade route people stand with their arms outstretched, yelling, "Moon pie! Moon pie!" at the tops of their lungs and leaping to catch these treats.

Visitors walk along the deck of the USS Alabama, *which saw action during World War II.*

The wildlife refuge offers a rich array of beachside and wilderness trails along which visitors can see pelicans, bobcats, and alligators.

In Mobile Bay, just east of the city, is the USS *Alabama* Battleship Memorial Park. The *Alabama* is an enormous ship that carried 2,500 crewmen into battle during World War II. Anchored nearby, the *Drum* is a submarine that was also used during World War II. Both vessels are open to the public, so visitors can climb up to the *Alabama*'s two-story observation deck and explore the long, low-ceilinged hallways that wind through the narrow interior of the *Drum*.

"It's hard not to be moved by all the memories here in Mobile," says a visitor from Anniston. "It makes you think about all the things the people in our state have been through over the years. We've fought for change and for freedom again and again—against foreign rulers, against slavery, against laws that weren't fair. But somehow, we've always managed to preserve the things that were beautiful and true from our past. And I hope we always will."

THE FLAG: *The Alabama flag, which is based on the Confederate battle flag, shows a red cross against a white background. It was adopted in 1895.*

THE SEAL: *Adopted in 1819, the state seal bears a map of Alabama that indicates the state's rivers, which were important to its economic development.*

State Survey

Statehood: December 14, 1819

Origin of Name: From the Alibamu Indians, whose name means "I clear the thicket"

Nickname: Heart of Dixie

Capital: Montgomery

Motto: We Dare Defend Our Rights

Bird: Yellowhammer

Flower: Camellia

Tree: Southern longleaf pine

Saltwater Fish: Tarpon

Mineral: Red iron ore

Rock: Marble

Horse: Racking horse

Freshwater Fish: Largemouth bass

Yellowhammer

Camellia

ALABAMA

The Alabama legislature adopted this as the official state song on March 3, 1931.

Words by Julia S. Tutwiler   **Music by Edna G. Gussen**

Game Bird: Wild turkey

Insect: Monarch butterfly

Gem: Star blue quartz

Highest Point: 2,407 feet above sea level, at Cheaha Mountain

Lowest Point: sea level, along the Gulf of Mexico

Area: 51,718 square miles

Greatest Distance North to South: 329 miles

Greatest Distance East to West: 210 miles

Bordering States: Mississippi to the west, Tennessee to the north, Georgia to the east, and Florida to the south

Hottest Recorded Temperature: 112 degrees Fahrenheit in Centreville on September 5, 1925

Coldest Recorded Temperature: −27 degrees Fahrenheit in New Market on January 30, 1966

Average Annual Precipitation: 56 inches

Major Rivers: Alabama, Black Warrior, Chattahoochee, Coosa, Mobile, Perdido, Tallapoosa, Tennessee, Tombigbee

Major Lakes: Eufaula, Guntersville, Martin, Pickwick, Weiss, Wheeler, Wilson

Trees: cedar, cypress, hemlock, hickory, oak, pine, poplar, sweet gum

Wild Plants: aster, azalea, dogwood, Dutchman's-breeches, goldenrod, mountain laurel, orchid, rhododendron

Animals: alligator, bear, bobcat, deer, gray fox, mink, opossum, rabbit, raccoon, red fox, skunk

Birds: cardinal, duck, flycatcher, goose, heron, mockingbird, osprey, swallow, whip-poor-will, wild turkey

Fish: bass, bream, buffalo fish, catfish, crappie, garfish, flounder, mackerel, mullet, red snapper, tarpon

Endangered Animals: Alabama beach mouse, Alabama cavefish, Alabama cave shrimp, Alabama redbelly turtle, American peregrine falcon, Anthony's riversnail, black clubshell, boulder darter, cracking pearlymussel, gray bat, Gulf moccasinshell, Indiana bat, oval pigtoe, oyster mussel, pink mucket, red-cockaded woodpecker, tulotoma snail, West Indian manatee, wood stork

Redbelly turtle

Endangered Plants: Alabama canebrake pitcher plant, Alabama leather flower, gentian pinkroot, green pitcher plant, harperella, leafy prairie clover, Morefield's leather flower, pondberry, relict trillium, Tennessee yellow-eyed grass

TIMELINE

10,000 BCE First people arrive in present-day Alabama.

1400–1700 Four major groups develop: Cherokee, Chickasaw, Choctaw, and Creek or Musgogee.

1519 Spanish explorer Alonso Álvarez de Piñeda becomes the first European to see Alabama when he sails into Mobile Bay.

1540 Spaniard Hernando de Soto leads the first European expedition into the interior of Alabama.

1702 Mobile is founded.

1711 Fort Louis is moved to present-day Mobile, becoming Alabama's first permanent European settlement.

1783 At the end of the American Revolution northern Alabama becomes U.S. territory.

1795 Spain cedes most of present-day Alabama to the United States.

1817 Alabama Territory is established.

1819 Alabama becomes the twenty-second state.

1838 The U.S. government forces American Indians to leave Alabama and move west.

1846 Montgomery becomes the state capital.

1861 Alabama secedes from the Union and joins the Confederate States of America; the Civil War begins.

1864 The Union wins the Battle of Mobile Bay.

1865 The Civil War ends.

1868 Alabama is readmitted to the Union.

1881 Booker T. Washington organizes the Tuskegee Normal and Industrial Institute to educate African Americans.

1887 The first steel plant in the South is established in Birmingham.

1901 The state's sixth and present constitution is adopted.

1924 Construction is halted on Wilson Dam, the first dam on the Tennessee River.

1933 The Tennessee Valley Authority is created to control flooding and provide cheap electricity.

1955 Rosa Parks is arrested for refusing to give up her seat to a white passenger on a segregated bus, setting off the Montgomery bus boycott.

1963 George Wallace is inaugurated as governor and tries to block the integration of the University of Alabama; four black girls are killed in the bombing of the 16th Street Baptist Church in Birmingham.

1965 Martin Luther King Jr. leads a civil rights march from Selma to Montgomery.

1989 Kathryn Thornton, from Montgomery, becomes the first woman to fly on a military space mission, on the space shuttle *Discovery*.

1998 Dr. David Satcher, from Anniston, is appointed U.S. surgeon general.

2005 Birmingham native Condoleezza Rice is appointed U.S. secretary of state.

2007 Alabamian and Pulitzer Prize winner Harper Lee receives the Presidential Medal of Freedom for her novel *To Kill a Mocking Bird*.

ECONOMY

Agricultural Products: beef cattle, catfish, chickens, corn, cotton, eggs, peaches, peanuts, pecans, soybeans, strawberries

Manufactured Products: automobiles, chemicals, clothing, fertilizers, food products, paper products, steel, textiles, wood products

Peanuts

Natural Resources: coal, crushed stone, iron, limestone, marble, natural gas, oil, oysters, shrimp

Business and Trade: finance, shipping, real estate, wholesale and retail trade

CALENDAR OF CELEBRATIONS

Eagle Awareness Weekends Throughout January, bird lovers gather at Lake Guntersville State Park to watch magnificent bald eagles soar overhead.

Mardi Gras Mobile is home to the nation's oldest Mardi Gras celebration. Each year the town cuts loose with two weeks of parades and revelry before Ash Wednesday, the beginning of Lent.

Rattlesnake Rodeo The highlight of this March festival in Opp is the world's only rattlesnake race. You can enjoy games, arts and crafts, and educational programs about rattlesnakes.

Battle of Selma Reenactment Each April history buffs in Selma bring the Civil War's Battle of Selma to life.

Alabama Jubilee Hot Air Balloon Classic Colorful hot air balloons fill the sky during this May festival in Decatur.

Blessing of the Fleet Everyone in the fishing center of Bayou La Batre comes out for this May event, which features a parade of boats, oyster-shucking and crab-picking contests, pet shows, and plenty of seafood to eat. Seafood gumbo is especially popular.

Alabama Jubilee Hot Air Balloon Classic

Hank Williams Festival Fans from across the nation flock to the tiny town of Georgiana each June to hear the songs of this country music legend at his boyhood home.

W. C. Handy Music Festival Each August Florence celebrates the music of the Father of the Blues with a week filled with jazz, blues, and gospel concerts.

Cherokee Pow Wow and Green Corn Festival At this event honoring the region's American Indians, you'll hear rhythmic music, watch vibrant dancing, and admire tepees and jewelry. The celebration takes place in Turkeytown in September.

Tennessee Valley Old Time Fiddlers Convention Come to Athens in October for a weekend of toe-tapping music. In addition to fiddle contests, the convention also features harmonica, banjo, mandolin, and guitar competitions.

Gulf Shores National Shrimp Festival More than 300,000 people descend on Gulf Shores in October to walk the sandy beaches and eat their fill of seafood. They also enjoy music, arts booths, and a sand sculpture contest.

National Peanut Festival George Washington Carver, the man who invented hundreds of uses for the peanut, spoke at the first National Peanut Festival in 1938. Today, this November event in Dothan features peanut recipe contests, livestock shows, and lots of fun and games.

Gulf Shores National Shrimp Festival

Christmas on the River Each December in Demopolis a glowing parade of boats decorated with lights brightens the night as it travels down the Tombigbee River.

STATE STARS

Hank Aaron (1934–   ), a Mobile native, held the major league record for career home runs until Barry Bonds broke it in 2007. Aaron crushed Babe Ruth's legendary record of 714 in 1974 and ended his career with 755. He is also the all-time major league leader in runs batted in, extra base hits, and total bases. Aaron spent most of his career with the Braves, at first in Milwaukee and later in Atlanta.

Hank Aaron

A quiet, consistent player, he led the league in home runs four times and hit at least thirty in a season fifteen times. During his long career he played in twenty-four All-Star Games. Aaron was elected to the National Baseball Hall of Fame in 1982.

Ralph Abernathy (1926–1990) was a Baptist minister and civil rights leader who was Martin Luther King Jr.'s closest associate in the 1950s and early 1960s. Together they led the Montgomery bus boycott and helped found a civil rights organization called the Southern Christian Leadership Conference (SCLC). Abernathy was president of the SCLC from 1968 until 1977. He was born in Linden.

Tallulah Bankhead (1902–1968), an actor born in Huntsville, was the daughter of William Bankhead, a Democratic politician who eventually became the speaker of the U.S. House of Representatives. Bankhead left school at fifteen and moved to New York, where she quickly established herself as a brilliant theater actress. The New York Drama Critics' Circle named her the year's best actor for *The Little Foxes* in 1939 and *The Skin of Our Teeth* in 1942. Although she never enjoyed the same success in movies, with her raspy voice and sophistication, she made her mark in such films as *Lifeboat*.

Hugo Black (1886–1971), a U.S. Supreme Court justice, was a native of Harlan. Black became a lawyer and was eventually elected to the U.S. Senate. In 1937 he was appointed to the Supreme Court, where he became known for his unwavering support of personal liberties, such as freedom of speech.

Paul "Bear" Bryant (1913–1983) was the most successful college football coach in history. Bryant, who was born in Arkansas, attended the University of Alabama, where he later became an assistant coach. He coached at Maryland, Kentucky, and Texas A&M before settling in as head coach at Alabama from 1958 to 1982. Legendary for being strict and demanding, Bryant was also extremely successful. By the end of his career he had racked up 323 victories, more than any other college coach.

Truman Capote (1924–1984) was a writer famous for the novel *Breakfast at Tiffany's*, about a lively New York playgirl. Many people think his greatest triumph was what he called his "nonfiction novel," *In Cold Blood*. It is a dark and disturbing account of a multiple murder in a small Kansas town. Capote, who was born in New Orleans, Louisiana, and spent his early years in Monroeville, Alabama, often delved into his southern background in his writing.

George Washington Carver (1864–1943) was a botanist who spent much of his career teaching at Alabama's Tuskegee Normal and Industrial Institute, a school for blacks in Tuskegee, Alabama. Carver, who was born in Missouri, became the director of the Department of Agricultural Research at Tuskegee Institute in 1896. Carver spent the rest of his life there doing agricultural research. He discovered hundreds of products that could be made from such local plants as sweet potatoes and peanuts. He also developed a better type of cotton and ways to improve soil.

Paul "Bear" Bryant

Nat King Cole (1919–1965) was a singer beloved for his smooth, rich voice. Cole was an outstanding jazz pianist of the 1940s. In 1944 his King Cole Trio had its first big hit with "Straighten Up and Fly Right." Later hits included "Mona Lisa" and "Unforgettable." In the 1940s Cole was the only African American with his own commercial network radio show, and in 1956 he became the second African American to have his own national television program. He was born in Montgomery.

William Crawford Gorgas (1854–1920), a doctor born in Mobile, was a pioneer in the control of such deadly diseases as yellow fever, malaria, and bubonic plague. Gorgas joined the army and in 1898 was sent to Havana, Cuba, to try to control a yellow fever epidemic. He was not able to control the epidemic until it was understood that the disease was spread by mosquitoes. By eliminating places where mosquitoes could breed, Gorgas freed Havana from the disease. He later did the same thing in Panama, where disease was slowing the construction of the Panama Canal.

W. C. Handy (1873–1958) was a composer and trumpet player known as the Father of the Blues. Handy began his career as a performer and a teacher. By 1907 he had begun composing. While traveling through the Mississippi Delta, Handy heard the blues for the first time. He later wrote such classics as "St. Louis Blues" and "Beale Street Blues," which brought the blues its first international recognition. Handy grew up in Florence.

Helen Keller (1880–1968) was an author and lecturer who lost both her sight and her hearing before age two. Eventually her teacher,

Nat King Cole

Anne Sullivan, found ways to teach her to communicate. Keller learned to read braille, to type with a special typewriter, and to speak. After graduating from Radcliffe College in 1904, she became an advocate for the blind and people with other disabilities. The play *The Miracle Worker* is based on Sullivan's experiences with Keller. Keller was born in Tuscumbia.

Dr. Martin Luther King Jr. (1929–1968) was the preeminent leader of the civil rights movement of the 1950s and 1960s, renowned for promoting nonviolent protest. King was born in Atlanta, Georgia, and became a Baptist minister. In 1954 he became the pastor of a church in Montgomery, Alabama, where he began his career as a civil rights leader. King's mesmerizing speeches, idealism, and dignity made him a national figure. In 1957 he helped found the Southern Christian Leadership Conference, a leading civil rights organization. He is perhaps best remembered for his "I have a dream" speech, delivered during the 1963 March on Washington. King, who won the 1964 Nobel Peace Prize, was assassinated in 1968.

Harper Lee (1926–   ) is a writer whose only novel, *To Kill a Mockingbird*, earned a Pulitzer Prize and was made into a successful movie. The book, which is set in a small Alabama town much like Lee's native Monroeville, concerns a lawyer who is defending a black man accused of a crime he did not commit. The novel was acclaimed for dealing with ideas about prejudice and heroism while also providing an insightful look at southern culture. Lee was awarded the Presidential Medal of Freedom in 2007.

Helen Keller

Joe Louis (1914–1981), who was born in LaFayette, was the world heavyweight boxing champion from 1937 to 1949. In 1936 Louis, who was nicknamed the Brown Bomber, lost to the German Max Schmeling. The Nazi regime in power in Germany at the time viewed Schmeling's victory as evidence of the superiority of whites. But when Louis beat Schmeling in a rematch in 1938, Americans celebrated and Louis became an inspirational figure during World War II. During his career Louis won sixty-eight of his seventy-one bouts.

Willie Mays (1931–   ), who was born in Westfield, is perhaps the greatest baseball player ever. Mays began his career with a bang, leading the New York Giants to the 1951 National League pennant, earning the Rookie of the Year Award, and winning legions of fans with his hustle and intelligence. Remarkably versatile, Mays was the first player to hit 300 home runs and steal 300 bases in his career. He ended his career with 660 home runs, the fourth highest career total. An amazing center fielder, Mays was famous for his spectacular catches and exceptionally strong and accurate throws. In 1964 Mays became the first African-American captain of a major league team. He was elected to the National Baseball Hall of Fame in 1979.

Alexander McGillivray (c.1759–1793) was a Creek Indian leader whose father was Scottish and mother was Creek and French. Born near what is now Wetumpka, he spent his early childhood living with the Creeks before being educated with whites in South Carolina. A skilled diplomat, McGillivray worked to unite the various Indian nations against white settlers, who were taking more and more of their land.

Willie Mays

Jesse Owens (1913–1980), a legendary track and field star, set eleven world records during his career. In one incredible afternoon in 1935, he broke three world records and tied another. At the Olympics in Berlin, Germany, the following year, Owens won four gold medals—in the 100-meter dash, the 200-meter dash, the long jump, and the 400-meter relay—embarrassing the German leader Adolf Hitler, who believed whites were superior to blacks. Owens was born in Oakville.

Satchel Paige (1906–1982) was one of the greatest pitchers in baseball history. When Paige began playing ball, African Americans were barred from the major leagues, so Paige spent most of his career in the Negro leagues. Paige's power and consistency are legendary. It is said that in 1934, he won 104 out of 105 games. Paige didn't get the chance to play in the major leagues until 1948, when he was more than forty years old. That year he joined the Cleveland Indians, leading them to a World Series victory. Paige, who was elected to the National Baseball Hall of Fame in 1971, was born in Mobile.

Rosa Parks (1913–2005) was a civil rights activist who set off the Montgomery bus boycott in 1955 when she was arrested after refusing to give up her seat on a bus to a white passenger. As a result of Parks's case the U.S. Supreme Court ruled segregation on public transportation to be unconstitutional. Parks was born in Tuskegee and attended Alabama State Teacher's College. She became active in the National Association for the Advancement of Colored People, a leading civil rights organization, and in 1943 became the secretary of the Montgomery branch. After the boycott Parks remained active in the civil rights movement.

Condoleezza Rice (1954–) was
appointed as the sixty-sixth U.S.
secretary of state and was born in
Birmingham. She lived in Alabama
until she entered high school. Then
her family moved to Colorado, where
Rice eventually entered the University
of Denver, at which she earned a
bachelor's degree in political science
and later a doctoral degree in the
same field, with a specialization in
Russia and Czechoslovakia. She once
wanted to be a concert pianist and,
although this dream did not come
true, she continues to play the piano.
She also speaks several different
languages. She was the provost of
Stanford University in California before becoming involved in politics.
From 1989 until 1991 she worked for President George Bush as the
director of Soviet and East European Affairs. Then, when President
George W. Bush took office, Rice worked as his national security advi-
sor (2001–2005). In 2005 Bush appointed her as his secretary of state.

Condoleezza Rice

Julia Tutwiler (1841–1916) was a social reformer who fought for
girls' education and for prison reform. She helped to establish girls'
schools and to convince the University of Alabama to admit
women. She also wrote the words to the Alabama state song.
Tutwiler was born in Tuscaloosa.

Robert Van de Graaff (1901–1967) was a physicist who invented a particle accelerator that is used in nuclear physics. His Van de Graaff generator has also been used in medicine to treat cancer. Van de Graaff was born in Tuscaloosa and attended the University of Alabama.

George Wallace (1919–1998), a four-term Alabama governor, was born in Clio. During his first term as governor Wallace became famous for his support of racial segregation. In 1963 he personally tried to block black students from entering the University of Alabama. Wallace ran for president as an independent in 1968 on a platform opposing desegregation and won in five states. In 1972, while again campaigning for president, he was shot and became paralyzed. In his later years Wallace changed his position on segregation.

Booker T. Washington (1856–1915) was the most prominent African American of the late nineteenth century. Washington had been born a slave in Virginia. After the Civil War he attended the Hampton Institute in Virginia, where he later became a teacher. In 1881 he was hired to organize the Tuskegee Normal and Industrial Institute, a vocational college for blacks in Alabama. At the school Washington emphasized practical training that would ensure African Americans could secure good jobs. Washington promoted a conservative view about civil rights, arguing that blacks needed to improve themselves by gaining economic self-reliance and job skills before they could expect to be granted equal rights. He remained president of Tuskegee until his death.

Dinah Washington (1924–1963), an exceptionally versatile jazz and blues singer, was born in Tuscaloosa. Washington could use her high, clear voice to express desperate sadness, rousing joy, and every emotion in between. She had her biggest hit in 1959 with "What a Difference a Day Makes."

Hank Williams (1923–1953) was one of the greatest and most influential country music singers ever, famous for such songs as "I'm So Lonesome I Could Cry" and "Your Cheatin' Heart." Williams was born in Mount Olive. While still a teenager, he was already leading a popular band in Montgomery. In 1949 his first performance at the Grand Ole Opry went over so well that he sang six encores. With their direct lyrics expressing intense emotions, his songs dominated the country music charts for the next few years. But Williams led a troubled life, suffering from alcoholism and other problems. He died of a heart attack at age twenty-nine.

TOUR THE STATE

Birmingham Civil Rights Institute (Birmingham) The moving history of African Americans' struggle for equal rights is told at this museum using film, music, and storytelling.

Alabama Sports Hall of Fame (Birmingham) This site is filled with memorabilia from the careers of Jesse Owens, Joe Louis, Hank Aaron, and many other Alabama sports greats.

Birmingham Zoo Look a Siberian tiger in the eye, watch golden spider monkeys cavort, and admire how elegantly huge polar bears glide through the water at one of the largest zoos in the Southeast.

Ave Maria Grotto (Cullman) This fascinating site contains miniature replicas of 150 churches and shrines from throughout the world. A monk named Brother Joseph Zoettl built them over the course of fifty years, using everything from semiprecious stones to soup cans.

Wheeler National Wildlife Refuge (Decatur) More than three hundred bird species pass through this refuge at some point during the year. Telescopes have been set up so you can see the birds without frightening them away. The refuge also includes scenic walking trails and picnic spots.

Ave Maria Grotto

U.S. Space and Rocket Center (Huntsville) The world's largest space museum is also the most visited tourist attraction in Alabama. You can wander among rockets and other spacecraft, watch films taken by astronauts in space, and take a bus tour through NASA's Marshall Space Flight Center, where you might see mission control and space shuttle test sites.

Ivy Green (Tuscumbia) At the childhood home of Helen Keller you'll hear the extraordinary story of how she learned to communicate despite being blind and deaf. You'll even see the pump where she learned her first word, water.

Alabama Music Hall of Fame and Museum (Sheffield) Exhibits, recordings, and memorabilia tell the story of great Alabama musicians, from Hank Williams to Nat King Cole.

W. C. Handy Home and Museum (Florence) Here you can see the log cabin where the Father of the Blues was born, along with handwritten music, photographs, and the piano on which he composed "St. Louis Blues."

Russell Cave National Monument (Bridgeport) Nine thousand years ago the ancestors of modern American Indians lived in this cave in northeastern Alabama. Today, you can view the cave and some of the pottery, tools, and other artifacts that have been found there.

DeSoto State Park (Fort Payne) This park features a spectacular scenic drive, hiking trails, and the lovely 100 foot DeSoto Falls.

Horton Mill Covered Bridge (Gadsden) This picturesque bridge is 70 feet above the Black Warrior River. No other covered bridge in the nation rises as high above the water.

Gaineswood (Demopolis) One of the most beautiful mansions in the South, this house boasts a ballroom with gigantic columns and mirrored walls, glass domes in the ceiling, and original furnishings.

Dexter Avenue King Memorial Baptist Church (Montgomery) Martin Luther King Jr. became a national figure while he was the pastor of this church during the 1950s. A highlight of the church tour is a mural that depicts events in King's life and the civil rights movement.

First White House of the Confederacy (Montgomery) Jefferson Davis and his family lived in this house in the early days of the Confederacy, before the capital was moved to Richmond, Virginia. Today, it houses items that once belonged to the Davis family and furnishings from that era.

Bellingrath Gardens and Home (Theodore) These gorgeous gardens include more than 250,000 azalea plants, as well as camellias, water lilies, dogwoods, and so many other flowering plants that there are always spectacular blooms, no matter what the season.

Gulf State Park (Gulf Shores) Miles of white-sand beaches lure sunbathers, while the waters beckon swimmers, fishing enthusiasts, and surfers. The park also boasts freshwater lakes perfect for fishing and canoeing and trails through pine forests that appeal to hikers and bikers.

Bellingrath Gardens

Fort Morgan (Gulf Shores) This star-shaped fort was built in the early nineteenth century and remained in use through World War II. Besides touring the fort, you can visit its museum, which is filled with military artifacts.

USS *Alabama* (Mobile) Exploring this World War II battleship will give you a feel for what life was life for its crew of 2,500.

FUN FACTS

You might think the people of Enterprise in southeastern Alabama would hate the boll weevil after the insect destroyed two-thirds of the region's cotton crop in 1915. But instead they erected a monument to the weevil, because the pest forced them to grow other crops, including peanuts and corn, which brought the region greater prosperity.

In 1910 the world's first flying school was established in Montgomery by aviation pioneers Wilbur and Orville Wright.

Although today Mardi Gras is more often associated with New Orleans, the first Mardi Gras celebration in North America was held in Mobile in 1703.

Find Out More

You can find out a lot more about Alabama at your local library or on the Internet. Here are a few suggestions to get you started.

GENERAL STATE BOOKS

Philipson, Claire Leila. *Alabama*. British Columbia, Canada: Whitecap Books, 2007.

Somervill, Barbara A. *Alabama*. New York: Children's Press, 2008.

SPECIAL-INTEREST BOOKS

Aaron, Hank. *I Had a Hammer: The Hank Aaron Story*. New York: Harper Perennial, 2007.

Asby, Ruth. *Rosa Parks: Courageous Citizen*. New York: Sterling Publishing, 2008.

Barker, Jay. *University of Alabama Football Vault: The Story of the Crimson Tide, 1892–2006*. Atlanta, GA: Whitman Publishing, 2007.

Tingle, Tim. *Walking the Choctaw Road*. El Paso, TX: Cinco Puntos Press, 2005.

Alabama Department of Archives & History

www.archives.state.al.us

This is the official online register of the state of Alabama. It includes basic historical information about the state, descriptions of government offices, and up-to-date lists of government officials, as well as many facts and statistics about the state.

Alabama Government

www.alabama.gov/portal/index.jsp

This is the official site of the state government, on which you can find information about the governor, senators, and state representatives, as well as school details.

Alabama Tourism

www.touralabama.org

The Alabama Bureau of Tourism's Web site keeps you informed about special events in the state and provides interesting virtual tours of some of the states' most beautiful sights.

Alabama Facts

www.ipl.org/div/stateknow/al1.html

This is a fun site, filled with interesting details about Alabama as well as lots of links to other Web sites about Alabama.

Index

Page numbers in **boldface** are illustrations and charts.

David Shirely grew up in Tupelo, Mississippi. He has written many books for young people, including a biography of Alabama sports legend Satchel Paige and *Mississippi* for the Celebrate the States series. He enjoys visiting his family in Birmingham, Alabama.

Joyce Hart has never lived in Alabama, though she has lived in the Deep South, in Charleston, South Carolina. She remembers seeing cotton fields, spying parks filled with blooming azalea, and feeling the hot breath of the southern sun on her face. She also remembers visiting Mobile while on a road trip and enjoying the refreshing waters of the bay. She now lives in the Pacific Northwest and dreams of those warm memories, especially during Washington's rainy winters.